THE HEAVENS ARE
CLEFT ASUNDER

THE HEAVENS ARE CLEFT ASUNDER

by

HUSCHMAND SABET

GEORGE RONALD
OXFORD

George Ronald, Publisher
46 High Street, Kidlington, Oxford OX5 2DN

This translation into English of *Der Gespaltene Himmel*
is published by arrangement with Verbum-Verlag GmbH
Original German-language edition © Copyright Verbum-Verlag GmbH
Stuttgart 1967
This translation © George Ronald 1975

ALL RIGHTS RESERVED

EXTRACTS FROM THE FOLLOWING WORKS
PUBLISHED IN THE UNITED STATES OF
AMERICA REPRINTED BY PERMISSION:

Alfred North Whitehead, *Science and the Modern World*, Copyright 1925 by Macmillan Publishing Co. Inc., renewed 1953 by Evelyn Whitehead. By Bahá'u'lláh: *Gleanings from the Writings of Bahá'u'lláh*, Copyright © 1952 by National Spiritual Assembly of the Bahá'ís of the United States; *The Kitáb-i-Íqán*, 2nd edn., Copyright © 1950 by National Spiritual Assembly of the Bahá'ís of the United States. By Shoghi Effendi: *God Passes By*, Copyright © 1944, 1971, 1974 by National Spiritual Assembly of the Bahá'ís of the United States; *The Promised Day Is Come*, Copyright © 1941, 1961 by National Spiritual Assembly of the Bahá'ís of the United States; *The World Order of Bahá'u'lláh*, Copyright © 1938, 1955, 1974 by National Spiritual Assembly of the Bahá'ís of the United States. Gerhard Szczesny, *The Future of Unbelief*, English translation, Copyright © 1961 by George Braziller, Inc.

Cased edition   ISBN 0 85398 055 1
Paper edition   ISBN 0 85398 056 X

*Printed by Billing & Sons Limited
Guildford and London*

ACKNOWLEDGEMENTS

This is the first English edition of my book, *Der Gespaltene Himmel*, which was published in Stuttgart in 1967. The text has been revised in certain respects, and it is hoped that these alterations, which are not many, have improved the book.

I wish to express my sincere gratitude to those who gave me special help in preparing this English edition: to Mr. Oliver Coburn who made the initial translation and read the proofs; to Mr. A. Q. Faizi and Mrs. Betty Reed for encouragement and valuable editorial suggestions; to Mrs. Beatrice Ashton who reviewed the translation, particularly in respect to its accurate presentation of the history and teachings of the Bahá'í Faith; to Mrs. Marion Battke and Mr. Achim Battke who also reviewed the translation; to my dear wife, Mrs. Ursula Sabet, and to Miss May Hofman, Mr. Mark Hofman, and Miss Claude Hunziker who consulted and advised me on doubtful points; to Miss Mary K. Perkins and Mrs. Hélène Momtaz Neri for assistance with the bibliography and certain translations of German texts; to Mr. Rustom Sabit for reading proofs; and, above all, to my editor, Mrs. Marion Hofman, without whose efforts this work could not now be presented.

Full details are given in the references and bibliography for the sources quoted. Unless otherwise noted in the references, Mr. Coburn has translated the quotations from German texts. Quotations from *The Koran* (*Qur'án*) are in the J. M. Rodwell translation, published in the Everyman's Library series.

I am much indebted to the several authors and publishers who have permitted me to quote from their copyright publications. Full acknowledgement is given in the bibliography to these publishers, their authors and titles. The Authorized Version of the Holy Bible is Crown Copyright and extracts used are with permission.

The jacket design is by John Jago, inspired by 'The Ancient of Days' by William Blake.

Finally, may I commend the various titles listed in the bibliography to the reader who may wish to look more deeply into the themes and subjects of this book.

CONTENTS

FOREWORD xi

INTRODUCTION xiii

I HAS RELIGION FAILED?

The decline of Christianity 1
Christianity and science 6
Charity and tolerance 7
Christianity and social problems 9
The claim to absolute truth and the change in cosmology 10
Demythologizing 12

II THE RELIGION OF UNITY

The birth of a new revelation 16
Bahá'u'lláh's mission and teaching 18
The 'Sun of Truth' 22
The spread of the new teaching 23

III THE OTHER FUTURE

War and peace 24
The spiritual transformation of humanity 29
Science and world peace 30
Peace on earth 31

CONTENTS

IV 'THE WALLS THAT DIVIDE US DO NOT REACH TO HEAVEN'

The 'Heathen'	37
Rise and development of Islám	38
The decline of Islám	45
The seeds of understanding	45
The Bahá'í Faith in the light of critical analysis	48

V THE NEW EARTH

Man's progress towards unity	55
Science and technology are changing the world	56
A new era	64

VI THE HERALD

Life and work of the Báb	69
The new teachings	76
Developments in Islám after the Bábí Revelation	78
The unfolding of the Bahá'í Faith	79

VII GOD'S COVENANT FULFILLED

No visible limits	82
Bahá'u'lláh's eldest son	83
Bahá'u'lláh proclaims his mission	85
Bahá'u'lláh's exile	86
'Abdu'l-Bahá: The Centre of the Covenant	88

VIII CHRIST

Jesus and Christendom	94

The Qur'án and the Christology of the Church	95
Man and the Manifestations of God	97
The Revealers' testimony about themselves	101
The station of the Revealers of God	105
The Revelation of God and theologians	109
Christ: The 'Essence of Being'	110
Sin and redemption	110

IX THE NEW HEAVEN

The most important message of the Gospels	120
The false Prophets	123
The Messianic expectation	124
Bahá'u'lláh's claim	125
The concept of 'heaven'	128
Bahá'u'lláh: The Promised One of all religions	132

CHRONOLOGICAL TABLE	139
BIBLIOGRAPHY	144
REFERENCES AND NOTES	148

In the Name of God, the Compassionate, the Merciful

When the Heaven shall cleave asunder,
And when the stars shall disperse,
And when the seas shall be commingled,
And when the graves shall be turned upside down,
Each soul shall recognise its earliest and its latest actions.

Qur'án, lxxxii: 1–5

FOREWORD

by ALESSANDRO BAUSANI

*Head of the Department of Islamic Studies
at the University of Rome*

THE prevalence of a futile, purely intellectual and ineffective attitude is one of the typical characteristics of our modern Western world, which bars the way leading to effective world unity, world peace, and the harmonious functioning of any form of world organization. We need something simple, moving both heart and mind—we need a *religion*.

In this book Huschmand Sabet shows convincingly how such a religion for our time does not have to be invented; it exists and has already existed for over a hundred years. Like almost all other religions, it came from the East: it was born in Persia. Does a modern world still need religion? Has Christianity failed? What are the practical possibilities of the other older religions? Why is the Bahá'í religion different from the rest?

The author, as an engineer with a strong sense of the practical, does not lose himself in the subtleties of theological exposition. Instead, with a simplicity and clarity characteristic of the 'rational faith' which Bahá'u'lláh demands of his followers, he outlines the programme for concrete and comprehensive unity in the light of the Bahá'í religion, especially in its relation to the hopes and expectations of present-day Christianity.

Many traditionally-minded people may find the book challenging; but to open-minded seekers for truth it will give food for thought. They are more numerous, and their numbers are growing all the time, in a world whose inhabitants are beginning to lose faith completely in the old pessimistic religions, as well as in a pseudo-optimistic atheism.

INTRODUCTION

'In the beginning God created the heaven and the earth . . .' —thus begins the biblical account of the Creation. Since this statement was first proclaimed to mankind, two words from it have lost none of their cardinal importance in theology, nor has it ever been possible to find substitutes for them. They are the concepts 'God' and 'heaven'.

Jewish and Christian theology cannot be imagined without the concept of 'heaven'; but it is firmly rooted also in Islám and the other great religions.

The 'new heaven', picture of a longed-for future outlined by John of Patmos in his revelations and visions, unites believers of all the great religions. They share the Messianic expectation that a Buddha, a Messiah, a Spirit of Truth, a S̲h̲áh-Bahrám or a Mihdí, will by his coming or his return create a 'new earth' not made by man. Even those who feel no religious ties dream of a future order worth striving for with all their strength.

In our age, marked by great disappointments, world wars and genocide, as well as by astonishing successes in the scientific and technological fields, people on the whole have remained very 'down-to-earth'. Through a chain of processes, a 'new earth' has grown up before our eyes which makes our own age look very different from that of our fathers. But, unobserved and almost unobtrusively, in the 'heaven' of spirit and religion, there are also developments at work which justify the highest hopes.

I

HAS RELIGION FAILED?

'Ye shall know them by their fruits.'

Has religion failed? It is a very important question, which I shall try to answer carefully and without presumption. Although I hope to throw light on it by an objective historical investigation, I realize that my judgment will be influenced by my own view of the world.

For the historical investigation, I shall start by asking how far the promise of each religion has been realized compared to the full scope of its origins; in other words, how far the claim of its revelation has been fulfilled. My outlook is governed by two convictions. One is that 'The Purpose of the one true God . . . in revealing Himself unto men is to lay bare those gems that lie hidden within the mine of their true and inmost selves.'[1] This means that the Messenger of God is the true and perfect teacher, through whom the latent positive forces in man are revealed. This enables man to reach a higher stage of perfection, and only then can he find his way to true humanity. The second conviction is that such a revelation has taken place in our time.

Since we in the West are closest to Christianity, which in the minds of many has become the embodiment of religion, I shall define the subject more narrowly by asking: Has Christianity failed?

The decline of Christianity

Many eminent historians and serious theologians see the

most recent developments in Christianity as symptoms of a decline of unprecedented magnitude in the history of Christendom. In the crises of the past, people were still essentially believers; they remained under the domination of Church tradition. The troubles caused by human inadequacies and lust for power could be overcome.

Today the problem is different in kind. A great many people are no longer able to believe, even though they may retain their outward connection with the churches. Church institutions make intensive efforts, Christian leaders muster all their wisdom, Church congresses and synods try to adapt their rulings to the modern world's conditions; but none of this seems to make any difference. In their hearts, unwittingly and sometimes unconsciously, people are becoming estranged from religion. The sovereignty the Church possessed in the Middle Ages has completely disappeared. For large sections of the population the Church represents the past, and to many people its language is no longer comprehensible. For the most part, even professing Christians on closer inspection prove to be mere sympathizers, who are not believers but simply consider some Church doctrines true or at least 'a good thing to believe'. The unified Christian philosophy of the West has been replaced by new systems and ideologies which consider faith expendable or even harmful.

The history of the disastrous decline of Christianity, on a purely factual basis, may be sketched as follows: It was about a hundred years ago that the Pope was deprived of his secular power.* He had to accept abandonment by Italy,

---

* For many authors Christianity's decline begins with Paul, for others with Constantine, for others with the end of the Middle Ages. I do not go back to these earlier developments, because I believe that in the last hundred years a new dimension in the decline of Christianity can be observed.

even by Rome itself. A separation of State from Church was carried out in France and various other Catholic countries. In Mexico, indeed, the Church was subjected to severe persecutions. In Spain, the Austro-Hungarian Empire, and some Eastern European countries, the Church found its influence greatly reduced after the overthrow of monarchy, that constant prop of Catholicism in those countries. In Italy, Fascism developed, inflicting heavy blows on the Church at its very centre. Through the flood-tide of materialist ideologies the Church forfeited a great deal of respect, so that in countries like Italy, where Roman Catholicism was the state religion, as much as a third of the population accepted philosophies of thorough-going materialism. In Germany 150,000 Catholics a year sever their connection with the Church. The same picture can be seen in other countries as well. In Holland, between 1960 and 1966, the number of those who did not go to church almost doubled, from nineteen to thirty-three per cent of the population. In those six years, 1,700,000 persons must have decided to leave the Church. In Britain, between 1930 and 1968 the electoral roll of the Church of England fell by a third, from 3.7 million to 2.7 million. Only 5.6 per cent of the population took Easter Day Communion in the Anglican Church in 1968.

Nor can the Church be too happy even with some who have remained believers, for their faith is so blind and uncritical that, according to one Catholic theologian, they would just as readily accept any dogma presented to them, even if it said exactly the opposite of what it does now.[2]

As for the Protestant Church, it has gradually split into many different sects and schools, already numbering over one thousand. Thus the unity which Jesus required of his disciples has been lost. Jesus, indeed, once predicted such a development as a sign of his imminent return, saying that many would appear and proclaim, 'Lo, here is Christ; or, lo, he is there . . .'[3]

In Germany, for instance, the country of Luther, national socialism had a paralysing effect on the Protestant Church, from which it has still not recovered. There is now danger of a split which could shake it to its foundations, arising from the discrepancy between the results of recent theological research and the preaching of the Gospel in congregations. In fact, if the Church can survive it will be partly because the results produced by scholarly research on the life of Jesus are not made public.[4]

Authoritative theologians deny the Virgin Birth, declare Christ's miracles to be myth or legend, and dispute the divine inspiration of the Gospel texts. Even the Sermon on the Mount, it is claimed, does not originate from Jesus except for a few maxims. Whether it is a matter of his death on the cross, the resurrection, eternal life, his divinity and omniscience, or any other basic point of faith, there are always at least two diametrically opposed opinions. In these confrontations, one may often doubt the true belief and real Christianity of those involved in the dispute.

The Church hierarchy is silent, trying to postpone as long as possible the imminent split. The would-be priest in his theological examination must convincingly qualify much of the testimony in the Gospels or declare it legendary, so that he can be ordained and preach it afterwards to his congregation, often as an article of faith. A Mainz theologian writes: 'He neither rose on the third day, nor did he ascend to heaven forty days after the resurrection. Jesus's ascension, which has been commemorated by Christians for almost two thousand years and which has been described in millions of ways, never took place.'[5]

Catholic theologians follow these leads cautiously and discreetly about thirty years later. The result was anticipated by Ernst Troeltsch in 1898 when he summed up research into the life of Jesus: 'Gentlemen, everything is in a state of flux.'[6]

The frailty of ordinary people's attachment to their Church institutions in Germany was confirmed, and never disputed, in a magazine report with alarming statistics: only 0·9 per cent of baptized Protestants are regular church-goers. Even the more favourable statistics given elsewhere are at most only a few per cent higher.

One Protestant clergyman told me that the Church sets greater store by those who do not attend than by the regular Sunday church-goers, because the former are to be taken more seriously as members of society. Another Protestant theologian accuses his Church of ignoring spiritual problems of concern to everyone, especially the young. 'How long,' he asks, 'at all too many church conventions and Bible courses, do they think they can get away with the sterile and dogmatic assertion of long out-dated beliefs and a complacent anti-historical religiosity which neither Jesus nor the apostles ever preached?'[7]

In the Eastern Orthodox sphere of influence, the organized attack on Christianity and on religion in general has crippled the Church, killed a large number of its adherents, confiscated all its land, closed thousands of churches and communal buildings and used them for secular purposes, and tried to tear from people's hearts every shred of religious feeling. The events of the Second World War allowed the materialist ideology to extend its influence still further. In the East it has gained China with 700 million inhabitants, part of Korea, and Vietnam; in the West, the Baltic countries, Poland, Bulgaria, Rumania, Yugoslavia, Albania, Hungary, Czechoslovakia, East Germany and Cuba. In the rest of the world as well, religious disintegration has never gone so far as today. The attractions of existing religion have shown themselves to be weak indeed.

In the intellectual and moral spheres, too, the Church's authority is questioned. Less importance is accorded today to pronouncements made by religious hierarchies or congresses than to those made by scientists, which also have a greater effect in stirring people's consciences. This is shown among other things by the modest results of the second Vatican Council, which at first looked so promising. Where it was hoped that a united front could be formed with the other branches of Christianity, the differences of opinion within the Council proved so great that only skilful diplomacy enabled it to conclude, to general relief, without an open split between 'progressives' and 'conservatives'.

Christianity and science

We can see from history that Christianity has failed also in questions relating to philosophy and science. The failure began when Christian theology adopted the science and philosophy of the ancients as a basis for its religious cosmology. Eventually, towards the end of the Middle Ages, Christianity was well to the rear in intellectual development. The dynamic character of the primitive religion gradually disappeared, and even in questions of philosophy and science it became static, falling more and more behind the dynamics of a progressive age. Gerhard Szczesny, an atheistic humanist, author of a well-known book, *The Future of Unbelief*, writes: 'The history of the bitter struggle between Christian dogma and modern science is impressive evidence of the inevitable defeat of the spiritualistic cast of thought, and points up the fact that often an attempt is made to hold fast to a position by sheer force when actually it has long since been pre-empted by experience. The Church's condemnation of the Copernican theory, resulting in the trial of Galileo Galilei in 1616, was not retracted until 1835. But in time, observe, it was retracted. As soon as notions of belief begin clearly to run counter to experimental fact, more and more their power to persuade is lost and more and more they sink to the status of mere literature. They are either ignored, or among the pious are tacitly taken to be fables or metaphors, which may contain a "deeper sense", but in which no actuality resides. Although unquestionably there are still a great number of people who take at face value the creation of the world in six days . . . the transubstantiation of bread and wine into the body and blood of Christ, etc., the majority today are kept from openly declaring these teachings to be incredible and unacceptable only out of fear of public reprisal. The Roman Catholic Church's resolute insistence on absurd tenets of belief and its fairly recent reaffirmation of its basic contempt for reason through the elevation to dogma of the Assumption of the Blessed Virgin, in fact signify neither victory nor affirmation for Christian spiritualism. In truth they signify retreat. A man sticks all the harder to his position when he feels the ground giving way beneath his feet.'[8]

Christian theology, by holding to the philosophy of the ancients, has reinforced the spirit of intolerance in Christianity and contributed to narrow dogmatic thinking. Moreover, the Church's identification with the scientific and philosophical concepts of a particular era has in later times caused its many defeats in the scientific and philosophical fields.

Charity and tolerance

The Christian personal ethic is probably the highest and

most exalted known to history. Christ's teaching is not only love of our neighbour; he also urges us to love our enemy.

Why did this ethic not prevail in Christendom? Why is the history of Christianity quite largely a history of intolerance? Why in clashes with dissenters have the most fanatical and intolerant groups often triumphed?

Even during quarrels inside the Church these extremist groups have often determined developments. One need think only of the dogma of the Pope's infallibility (1870), to which many Catholic theologians today have added qualifications and reservations. With extremist forces in the ascendant, it became increasingly difficult to bridge the gap between the Church and dissenters or people of different faiths. A typical claim to absoluteness and exclusiveness won the day, and was made the central point of all religious discussions. Every doctrine and every individual were then measured by this criterion. Consequently one's 'neighbour' was either a believer or of the heathen. If a Messenger of God or the founder of a religion did not belong to the biblical order of prophets, he was simply declared a false prophet.

Even when Christian met Christian, the spirit of tolerance was very little in evidence. Think of the Thirty Years War, or of the millions of people burnt as witches in the Middle Ages and right up to the eighteenth century. As late as the seventeenth century, witch trials produced about a million victims; and we should bear in mind when considering numbers that during those three centuries Europe was far more sparsely populated than it is today. As for the Inquisition, historians give a figure of about ten million victims.

Pope John XXIII, it is true, showed a more tolerant attitude towards other religions. At Pentecost, for instance, when he was consecrating fourteen missionary bishops in St. Peter's, he said, 'The countries from which you come, and for which you are being consecrated, rightly preserve and honour the age-old heritage of their civilizations. The hidden beauties of those civilizations, studded with traces of revealed truth, if made the subject of more careful study, might prove of the utmost value in compiling a comprehensive history of Man's spiritual life.'[9]

Did this mean that everything said in past centuries about Buddhists and Muslims was wrong, and that the non-biblical religions, too, contained revealed truth? But how could that tally with the Church's historical development and Christianity's general attitude?

Christendom has not in fact been able to create a universal basis for tolerance, love, unity and peace. This role had to be taken over by humanism, and later by the State and democracy. These and not the Churches today ensure that religions and creeds do not curtail each other's rights. Time and again they have had to remind church authorities that all human beings have equal rights. That is why, strange as it may sound, the separation of State and Church has proved a great step forward in European spiritual life.

Christianity and social problems

Nor has Christianity been very fortunate in socio-economic matters and in settling the problems of our daily life. Its failure in this sphere has contributed to the development of the greatest idol known to human history—materialism in both its Western and its Eastern forms.

Neither Marx nor Engels intended to create a substitute for religion; but because the representatives of Christianity were so reactionary in their attitude to the needs of the age, socialism assumed a 'religious', even a 'messianic' hue, and the ground was thus indirectly prepared for the extremes of revolutionary communism. Since the religious leaders had nearly always given their blessing to those in power and to an unjust social order, the mass of working people had no alternative but to fight on two fronts: against the exploiting powers on the one hand, and on the other against the Church institutions which promised them a realm of justice in the next world but were not prepared by word or deed to relieve their poverty in this world or help them realize their just demands. The contention by many representatives of the Churches that the masses were de-christianized by the malice of certain philosophers, party officials or socialist theorists, is historically untrue; it confuses cause and effect.

The claim to absolute truth and the change in cosmology

Is Christianity, then, no longer a light in the darkness? In our present stage of knowledge has it no longer any inspiration to give? Why do we find it impossible, even with the best will in the world, to leap the unbridgeable abyss between what we know and what we are expected to believe? The question may be asked in general terms, going beyond Christianity: Why is it that at a particular era of human history a religion acts creatively and constructively, while in another its effect is inhibiting or even *destructive*?

This question touches religion in a very sensitive spot: it amounts to asking whether the truths expressed by each religion are to be considered absolute truths, everywhere and at all times. If the truth of each religion were the reflection of absolute truth throughout time, then logically it would always remain equally creative and dynamic. But history teaches that with religions, too, a development may be traced like that from spring to winter. When a new Messenger or Prophet of God appears, new creative powers are revealed, which cause positive changes everywhere. But over the centuries human shortcomings increase so much that the Sun of Truth is obscured by the clouds of human indolence, lust for power and intolerance; and a critical observer, even without malice, may conclude that all this is 'opium for the people'.

Moreover, our understanding of a religion's sacred writings, which were composed in the language of their age, is subject to continual revision and additions. But if there is a very long interval between the picture outlined in the Scriptures and the 'reproductions' by various theologians, then it is almost impossible to make out the old picture clearly without the mediating authority of a new Revealer.

In this context let us look, for instance, at the Creation story and the concepts of 'heaven' and 'earth', which in the Bible signify the two spheres of the universe. The structure of the world is envisaged as a house carried by the earth, its roof resting on pillars.[10] The earth is a flat disc, and heaven is the place of light; so it has sun, moon and stars fixed to it. Until modern times this picture was taken literally, and it still represents the way many uneducated people see the world, while theologians of the most varied shades try hard to interpret it in the light of new scientific findings. One is overcome by a feeling of sadness, remembering how for thousands of years millions and millions of serious and deeply religious people have clung to this literal picture and even made it the centre of their scientific and religious discussions.

On the other hand, we must ask which of the many interpretations of the Creation story most closely resembles the picture originally intended. One thing at least seems established: the story is not about nature and its problems but about questions of faith. In my view it points to a never-ending creative act by God, and gives the plan of history, wherein all created things receive God's salvation in increasing measure.

This, however, should lead us to recognize that the testimonies of the Bible are expressed in images tied to the era of their origin, which, as interpreted by theology and tradition, do not offer us any unconditionally certain and permanent insights. Many things, in fact, remain obscure, mysteries which can only be unravelled at some later period. The idea, too, of Christ's 'atonement', namely, that someone dies for the sins of others, is alien to our modern thinking and feeling. Even if one has been familiar with these ideas from early childhood, on closer reflection they still appear more like myths.

This basic difficulty has resulted in the forming of two theological schools within the Protestant Church. One of them—Karl Barth is its most eminent representative—takes over directly the Bible's statements and so puts Christ's atonement at the centre of its thinking.[11] This brand of theology maintains essentially that there is a complete separation of God and man, and between Christianity and all other religions. All man's efforts and actions in this world, all religions even, are thus rendered profane and valueless. Everything must derive its significance from the crucifixion of Jesus. But if, as claimed by the Protestant theologian Schrey, our modern consciousness is incapable of understanding Christ's atonement,[12] the ground is cut from under the feet of these theologians, even though many theological objections may remain. We cannot mentally put ourselves back two thousand years, in order to believe the same ideas as people held in that era. Our consciousness may be refined or perfected; it can never be reversed.

Demythologizing

This fact has prompted Bultmann to suggest demythologizing Christianity.[13] His school tries to present eternal truth by stripping the biblical imagery of its mythical guise. But how can one separate image and fact in such a way that the full content is preserved? For the interpretation is largely determined by our modern consciousness, a consciousness itself subject to change and progress.

The result of these reflections can be summed up in two sentences. First, a demythologizing process is essential for a new presentation of truth. Second, our modern scientific consciousness, however, is not capable of such a process. (Personally I find it open to question whether the efforts to provide a new theology in fact preserve Christianity or rather betray it.)

According to the Bible, such a capacity is to be found only in the Spirit of God. Paul writes, 'He will bring to light the hidden things of darkness', and speaks of a 'hidden wisdom' of God, a mystery which only the Spirit of God can reveal.[14] From the mouth of Daniel we hear: 'O my Lord, what shall be the issue of these things?' To which God replies: 'Go thy way, Daniel: for the words are closed up and sealed till the time of the end.'[15] Clearly, unless a new revelation unseals mythological truth, present-day attempts to solve the problems involved, however intensive, have no chance of success. But once the truth hidden in mythology has been revealed, we must also reckon with strong emotions being aroused and the spirit of opposition fighting bitterly against such revelation. We can observe this situation historically at the appearance of every Messenger of God and at the inception of every epoch-making idea of renewal. Religious writings of today show that the writers have become familiar with such ideas and possibilities and are trying to adapt to them.

'Christians have long since ceased to be the leaven,' said the German theologian Müller-Gangloff in a radio broadcast (in 1959), 'which could leaven the world, let alone a light to lighten the world . . .' And further: 'We cannot be too thorough in questioning our firmly set positions—even to asking . . . whether the Holy Spirit today has not deserted the Church and gone over to the heathen. Or, to put it even more bluntly: after the old Israel, which grew rigid in the Synagogue, and the new people of God, the Christians, who built the Church, is there today perhaps a third people of God—coming from the heathen, the Gentiles of our own time?'[16]

Such far-reaching questions put one in mind of Peter's prophecies, usually given quite a different interpretation. Considering the revolutionary events which will accompany the Lord's return, Peter said: 'But the day of the Lord will come as a thief in the night; in the which the heavens shall pass away with a great noise, and the elements shall melt with fervent heat, the earth also and the works that are therein shall be burned up.'[17]

Peter himself answered the question of what then was to happen to man, after these tremendous changes and the destruction of the heaven as envisaged by past religions and civilizations. He answered it with these glad tidings: 'Nevertheless we, according to his promise, look for new heavens and a new earth, wherein dwelleth righteousness.'[18] Although opposed to the ideas which have prevailed till now, perhaps these new heavens and this new earth may mean a religion in a new attire, which is to bring fulfilment by the mighty hand of God through His Revealer with the 'new name'—as promised in Isaiah and in the Book of Revelation.[19]

Arnold Toynbee sees this possibility in his own way: 'The historic religions, with their traditional forms of expression, are becoming outdated, and that is one of the reasons, I believe, why they have been losing their influence in recent times. But I also believe that men will not live without religion. Once we have been awakened to consciousness, we feel that we are strangers in this universe in which we have been placed. There is a burning desire within us to come into contact with the spiritual reality behind the universe, so as to achieve harmony with it.

'That is why I believe we must abandon the historic religions in their old and perhaps obsolete external forms, in order to fit them into new forms which correspond to their fundamental similarity, appropriate to us and to our age. That is a tricky and difficult undertaking. I believe we shall try to tackle it, because I believe that, in the world we are moving towards, we shall feel the same need felt by most earlier generations, the need for a religion to which we can offer our whole-hearted devotion.'[20]

As an editorial in the American journal *Christian Century* stated a few years ago: '. . . the highest duty which the church can render the nation today is to call the people to almighty God in prayer, that He will send a leader or leaders who will guide our thoughts in a wholly new direction and we will pray, night and day, that when that leadership appears, we will have the courage to follow it and not to crucify it.'[21]

II

THE RELIGION OF UNITY

The birth of a new revelation

IN our age we have the chance to witness something rare and wonderful: the birth and development of a revealed religion, which claims to be the universal religion of the future.

Its history began in 1844, when ʿAlí-Muḥammad, a twenty-five-year-old merchant from Shíráz in Persia, declared himself the herald of the Divine Will in our day and at the same time assumed the name 'Báb', that is, the 'Gate' to him whom God would later reveal* and to whom he would be 'subordinate in rank'.[1] The Báb was spared for only six years after his declaration. He was taken from prison to prison, until eventually, on 9 July 1850, at the hands of Persia's orthodox clergy, abetted by her rulers, he suffered a martyr's death.

The one whose coming had been foretold gathered round him the discouraged followers of the Báb and in 1863 declared himself the Promised One of all ages and religions. He called himself 'Baháʾuʾlláh', which means the 'Glory of God'. He confirmed his claim by countless writings and letters, which he addressed to believers, the clergy, and the rulers of the East and West. For forty years, until his death in 1892, he was an exile and a prisoner, finally in the penal colony of ʿAkká (or Acre, in Palestine), where his earthly remains were laid to rest.

* 'Him whom God shall make manifest', in the words of the Báb.

His eldest son, ʿAbbás Effendi, known under his spiritual name ʿAbdu'l-Bahá (literally, the 'Servant of Glory'), was in Bahá'u'lláh's testament appointed the 'Centre of the Covenant'* and the interpreter of his writings. ʿAbdu'l-Bahá too remained a prisoner until the Young Turks' Revolution in 1908. After his release he made journeys between 1911 and 1913 to Europe and the United States, where he expounded his father's teachings in churches, synagogues and religious gatherings of all kinds. In 1921, when ʿAbdu'l-Bahá died in Palestine, the religion founded by Bahá'u'lláh had already gained a footing in thirty-five countries. With the death of ʿAbdu'l-Bahá the 'Heroic Age' of the Bahá'í Faith ended. Now began a period which the Bahá'ís call the 'Formative Age'.† In his testament ʿAbdu'l-Bahá appointed his grandson, Shoghi Effendi, 'Guardian of the Cause of God', who, under the infallible protection of Bahá'u'lláh, became the only authorized interpreter of Bahá'í sacred writings.

In the thirty-six years of Shoghi Effendi's ministry Bahá'u'lláh's teaching was disseminated in over 250 countries, Bahá'í literature was translated into nearly 240 languages, and Bahá'í centres and communities grew up in 4,500 towns and villages.

---

* The one to whom the followers of Bahá'u'lláh were to turn for guidance.
† The Bahá'ís divide the Dispensation of Bahá'u'lláh into Heroic, Formative and Golden Ages. The first comprises the ministries of the Báb, Bahá'u'lláh and ʿAbdu'l Bahá, from 1844 to 1921. In the second, the administrative institutions of the Bahá'í Faith are being established in accordance with their instructions, and consolidated throughout the world, to give visible expression to the World Order founded by Bahá'u'lláh. In the Golden Age, which will succeed the Formative Age, the blessings of the spiritual unity of mankind will become visible in all spheres of human existence.

After the death of Shoghi Effendi in November 1957, the leadership of the religious community passed to the 'Hands of the Cause of God', whom he had appointed and finally designated 'Chief Stewards' of the Faith. In April 1963, exactly one hundred years after Bahá'u'lláh's declaration, the Universal House of Justice was elected by the representatives of the whole Bahá'í world.

This institution, founded by Bahá'u'lláh, is the supreme administrative authority of the Faith and directs, through the national and local Spiritual Assemblies, the affairs of the world-wide Bahá'í community. Bahá'u'lláh has invested it with specific powers and authority. Its seat is in Haifa.

Bahá'u'lláh's mission and teaching

The axis round which all Bahá'u'lláh's teachings revolve is unity. He teaches the existence and the unity of a personal God and the unity of the Messengers of God, who, although living under different conditions and with teachings adapted to different peoples' powers of understanding, have always proclaimed the same Word of God and the same truth. According to Bahá'u'lláh, the plan of Divine Revelation comprises also the religions which are not in the biblical series of revelations, such as Buddhism, the religion of Zoroaster, Hinduism and Islám.

Through his mission Bahá'u'lláh, within the never-ending revelation of God, will establish the unity of all mankind and found a divine world civilization. To live and work for the salvation of all humanity is the highest and noblest task of every Bahá'í.

Bahá'u'lláh teaches that the Revealers of God are endowed with absolute divine authority and innate knowledge. Their revelations, however, are relative to the changing needs of the people of each age. Hence, two of Bahá'u'lláh's essential teachings are the 'relativity of religious truth' and 'progressive revelation'.

Many principles which the modern world calls its own are among the articles of Bahá'í belief: the independent and unfettered search for truth; the abandonment of all prejudices, religious, racial or national; the equal and best possible education of both sexes; the introduction of a universal auxiliary language and a universal script, as well as an internationally valid system of currency, weights and measures; also the promotion of the complementary nature and the harmony of science and religion, whereby science for the Bahá'í has above all a technological and 'discovering' task and religion a creative and constructive one. The Bahá'ís find a solution of the economic problem in efforts to reduce the extremes of wealth and poverty. The practice of a profession or trade based on service to humanity is the duty of every individual and such work has been accorded the status of divine worship by Bahá'u'lláh. All these principles were enunciated by Bahá'u'lláh over a hundred years ago.[2]

Bahá'u'lláh affirms that there *is* life after death and speaks of a unity between this world and the next.* The relation between the two is compared with the condition of human beings in the womb and in the world. The embryo develops eyes, ears and legs but cannot immediately see, hear and walk with them. In the same way we are called on to acquire spiritual qualities in this world, which will be our 'eyes, ears and legs' in God's worlds to come. Just as the pre-natal world has a unity with this world despite the limitations of the womb, one may speak of the unity of the spiritual world

---

* This unity of the worlds should not be understood as encouraging the use of psychic faculties. The reader is referred to Esslemont's *Bahá'u'lláh and the New Era*, pp. 177–9, for a statement of the Bahá'í view.

to come and of our present world which is characterized and restricted by the conditions of matter. Through prayers for them and good works we can promote the spiritual development of those who have discarded their earthly shell. On the other hand, our earthly development is influenced by the help of the departed, who are working with us today for the unity of all mankind.

In Bahá'u'lláh, the Bahá'ís see the fulfilment of the promises of all the historic religions. In his *Book of Certitude** he teaches the basic unity of religions. He shows that all the Holy Scriptures are completely in harmony with one another. This unity extends to the Messengers of God, who reflect divine reality like perfect mirrors. That is why the varied language of those who have spoken to humanity as men, as mediators and at the same time as living God,† should not lead us to deduce from their pronouncements a claim for the uniqueness or finality of any one of the historic religions. Such a claim would be opposed to recognition of the unity of religion, and would disregard the principle of further revelation to come, which has a special place in all the great religions.

The Bahá'ís are grateful and happy that they are in possession of no less than a hundred volumes of authentic writings by Bahá'u'lláh, many of which are preserved in the original in the Bahá'í archives at Haifa.

God, whose Being is beyond our perception, has sent Bahá'u'lláh to mankind, the Bahá'ís believe, in this dark hour of fate, to make known the divine intention of spiritual peace. This 'Most Great Peace' will be preceded by a political peace. Every organization which sets itself against the realization of the exalted aim of unity, whether it is a

---

* *Kitáb-i-Íqán.*
† See pp. 101–2.

religious, political or any other community, carries within it the seeds of its own destruction and disintegration. The spiritual unity of mankind is the essence of the divine plan, and human free will can do no less and no more than reduce or increase the tribulations and the time-span which separate us from those days. The Bahá'í Faith declares expressly that soon the maturity of mankind will succeed the turbulence and shocks of its youth and introduce a new epoch of peace. Thus we find in all Bahá'u'lláh's teachings, whether they concern individuals or the community, the starting points for potential maturity. The individual is given the duty of seeing with his own eyes and hearing with his own ears, of seeking independently after truth. Every Bahá'í is required to pass on Bahá'u'lláh's teaching to other seekers. Particular administrative functions, such as the care of the community, marriage ceremonies, and others, are assigned to the Spiritual Assemblies (bodies of nine honorary members elected annually).* The establishment of a paid priesthood is abolished. The sermon loses its importance in the service of God. In the Houses of Worship† sacred writings of the various religions are to be read aloud without human commentaries and interpretations.‡ Rites and man-made dogmas disappear; sacramental acts are no longer retained.

* The elections which precede the formation of Bahá'í institutions, from the Local Assemblies to the Universal House of Justice, are democratic, with the qualification that those elected are responsible to God and to their own consciences but not to the electors. Electioneering, nomination of candidates, or any attempt to influence the voters is incompatible with the spiritual character of Bahá'í elections and is forbidden.

† Houses of Worship have been erected in all continents. According to Bahá'u'lláh such Houses will come into being in every town and village, and will form the centres of spiritual and cultural life.

‡ Of course everyone is permitted in lectures, discussions and meetings of all kinds to express and develop his opinion freely. The fact that in the Houses of Worship no sermons are delivered and no explanations

The 'Sun of Truth'

The Revelation of God, on which man's development altogether depends, brings to bear upon mankind in two ways the positive forces and impulses which come from the Manifestations of God.* One is through the believers, who by personal transformation and gradual development of the new image of man and his ideals exert an ever increasing influence, regardless of all the obstacles to be overcome and all the sacrifices to be made. The second way is that the creative word of God's Messenger can so influence everything which happens on earth that his teachings become the guidelines for the development of all mankind, even before the majority of men and women have recognized the revelation, let alone accepted it as true.

In the Bahá'í Faith the Manifestation of God is often compared to the sun. When the sun appears on the horizon, it becomes bright not only where the sun's rays fall directly, but also where they do not find immediate access. All life on earth is dependent, in fact, on the sun's rays. Bahá'u'lláh has written: 'The Sun of Truth is the Word of God upon which depends the education of those who are endowed with the power of understanding and of utterance. It is the true spirit and the heavenly water, through whose aid and gracious providence all things have been and will be quickened.' And again: 'The whole world and whatever is therein are wholly dependent upon man and are manifested in him;

---

may be given, emphasizes that human opinions and conclusions should be more clearly separated from the Holy Scriptures. It also shows that human statements and commentaries do not have the authority reserved for the 'Word of God'.

* 'Manifestations of God' is the Bahá'í term for the ones who reveal the will of God to man. They are the Founders of the world religions.

while man himself owes his existence to the Day-star of the Word of God.'[3]

The Baháʼís believe, then, that every kind of intellectual, scientific and cultural progress is to be attributed directly or indirectly to the eternal and living Word of God. If the Sun of Truth ceased to shine, the human spirit would wither. This religious belief has also been confirmed recently by important thinkers and philosophers. Professor Arnold Toynbee, for instance, shows in his histories that every civilization has a religious basis, but that whereas the civilizations of the past have risen and then disappeared, religion has a progressive character.[4]

The spread of the new teaching

The Baháʼís work today throughout the world with a unique enthusiasm, free from denominational and party-political ties, for the realization of the aims set by Baháʼuʼlláh.

In the short history of this religion no less than twenty thousand believers have borne witness with their blood to the truth of their cause. Today, inspired by these martyrs, the Baháʼís everywhere are striving to bring Baháʼuʼlláh's glad tidings to seekers from all peoples, races and social classes.* For the Baháʼí Faith, which despite its rapid progress has only reached a small part of mankind, offers those who accept it the certainty and confidence that God has not left us alone in this fateful hour.

---

* The world-wide Baháʼí teaching activity and the development of the Baháʼí administrative order are made possible by the voluntary work and contributions of the Baháʼís. Only Baháʼís may contribute financially to the work of their Faith.

III

THE OTHER FUTURE

War and peace

IN the West there is an old saying, if you want peace, prepare for war. It has been applied to science and philosophy as well as politics. Bismarck, Darwin and Nietzsche—each in his fashion and in his own field—have declared this maxim valid. People used to think that the struggle for existence was one of nature's laws: the stronger must win, the weaker go to the wall. Wars have been regarded not only as inevitable but also as necessary for man's progress. Today opinions of this maxim are everywhere very divided.

Bahá'u'lláh spoke a hundred years ago of unity—the unity of God, of religions, of the Messengers of God, of the basic spiritual unity of mankind, and he stressed the need for universal peace. One of his sayings was: 'It is not his to boast who loveth his country, but it is his who loveth the world.'[1] Some may object that these or similar thoughts have been expressed before. Certainly; for at all times there have been noble men and women, and idealists who have stood for the highest human ideals, including the unity of mankind.

We must ask ourselves what is special about Bahá'u'lláh's words. When we study his writings closely, we are surprised how clearly in the middle of the nineteenth century he foresaw the mighty advances in science and technology which today bring men face to face with the alternatives: unite or perish. He was probably the only person at the time who did. He said: 'A strange and wonderful instrument exists in the earth; but it is concealed from minds and souls. It is an instrument which has the power to change the atmosphere of the whole earth, and its infection causes destruction.' He also stated: 'It is impossible to reform these violent, overwhelming evils unless the peoples of the world become united in affairs, or in one religion. Hearken ye unto the voice of this oppressed One, and adhere to the Most Great Peace!'[2] In one of his letters 'Abdu'l-Bahá referred to the above-mentioned words of Bahá'u'lláh—it was in the early days of aeronautics—and remarked that in 'the hands of men of lower material nature, this power would be able to destroy the whole earth'. He prayed that 'this force be not discovered by science until spiritual civilization shall dominate the human mind.'[3]

Eighty years later we hear the voice of scientists: 'We who sign this appeal are scientists from many countries, of various races, different creeds and different political convictions. But we all share the privilege of having been awarded the Nobel Prize.

'We have been happy to devote a life-time to the service of Science, for we think that Science is a way to a fuller life for mankind. But we are alarmed when realizing that it is this very Science which now provides man with the means of self-destruction.

'By total war and the use of now available weapons the world may become so infested with radio-activity that war would result in the destruction of whole nations, annihilating both neutrals and belligerents.

'Should the Big Powers engage in war, who can guarantee that it will not develop into such a deadly struggle? Thus any nation engaging in total war invites its own destruction and endangers the whole world.

'We do not deny it is the fear of these destructive weapons by which Peace is maintained at present in this world. Yet we think it extremely deceptive for any government to believe that fear of such weapons will, in the long run, prevent wars. On the contrary, fear and tensions have only too often led to the outbreak of wars. Likewise it also seems to us self-deception to imagine that minor conflicts could still be settled by employing the traditional weapons. No warring nation will, in times of extreme danger, deny itself the use of any weapons that scientific techniques can supply.

'Thus all nations must arrive at the decision voluntarily to renounce force as the last recourse in foreign policy. For they will cease to exist if they are not prepared to do so.'[4]

Some time ago a committee of German scientists, commissioned to look into the question of protection of the civilian population against nuclear weapons, produced a report to the effect that there was no real defence against a nuclear attack because the enemy could at far smaller cost completely frustrate the measures taken.

Bahá'u'lláh repeatedly admonished mankind, above all the peoples of the West, to practise 'moderation' in civilization. He advised rulers and governments to disarm, for otherwise the expenditure on armaments would reach proportions that would seriously disturb the ordered life of mankind. Today governments in East and West, those of the 'neutrals' too, and even the developing countries, spend between 25 per cent and 60 per cent of their revenue on armaments, about seven and a half million sterling pounds an hour. With that money houses could be built in a very short time for the inhabitants of a large city. Today more is spent within a few hours on armaments in 'peace-time' than a whole war cost a century ago. Admittedly considerable sums have lately been allocated for help to developing countries, which are supported by the World Bank and a great many national and international institutions. But on our shrunken planet, where everyone has become everyone else's neighbour, such behaviour is like that of a man who spends £10 a year storing up dynamite and explosives in case he has to blow up his neighbours' houses, but at the end of the year offers a shilling towards the most necessary repairs to those houses.

Science and technology have made unprecedented strides in the last century and a half, but the most impressive progress has been achieved in a dubious field, that of weapons and destruction. One reason why our age must be considered a turning-point in history is that for the first time man is able to jeopardize his own existence and, indeed, the existence of all life on this planet. The United States Secretary of Defence declared in 1958 that in a nuclear war 'between NATO and the Powers of the Warsaw Pact' 160 million Americans, 200 million Russians and the whole population of Western Europe would be killed. Scientists informed him that this prognosis was too optimistic: for a far smaller outlay than all the world's countries spend on armaments today, a 'Doomsday machine' could be constructed, they said, capable of destroying all human life in a matter of seconds. Hermann Kahn, theorist of nuclear war, said a few years ago that if he thought it worth while, he could no doubt make such a machine operational; fortunately he did not at the time consider this desirable. Dr. Linus Pauling, twice Nobel Prize winner, has written: 'For six billion dollars—one-twentieth of the amount spent on armaments each year by the nations of the world—enough Cobalt bombs could be built to ensure the death of every person on earth. . . . No matter what sort of protection were to be devised, it is highly unlikely that any human being would remain alive.'[5]

The cobalt bomb, however, is only one of the possibilities of extermination; various others are being discussed. Bertrand Russell has written: 'Imagine a world in which the sky is darkened by flights of Russian and American satellites returning, say once a day, and each capable of inflicting enormous slaughter. Would life be livable under such conditions? Would human nerves be capable of enduring them?'[6]

At least four times in the last fifteen years we have been near to world-encompassing disaster. In the next fifteen years there will be about another ten Powers capable of playing with a fire which can burn down our world. Twenty thousand times as much destructive energy as was used in the Second World War is waiting in the nuclear stores of the various countries for possible use. The situation becomes even more critical when one remembers that these annihilation weapons with their devastating effects could come into action not only by intention but also through human or mechanical error.

Even apart from this, men's activities do not seem to be guided by reason. Every year large amounts are spent on cancer research and health services. Far larger sums, however, are spent in order to destroy life. One out of every two of the earth's inhabitants can neither read nor write, although illiteracy could be completely eliminated with the amount which is spent in only twelve days on armaments. For every human being who has enough to eat, there are two who are starving. Yet the world could absorb and feed adequately several times its present inhabitants. Nor can we deny that in much of our behaviour we human beings are little better than animals. In all fields of life there are developments going on which endanger or actually harm mankind.

The spiritual transformation of humanity

The only chance left for humanity lies in a basic transformation embracing all spheres of life. Admittedly our present situation, which makes such a transformation essential, offers little ground for hope. Despite the resources granted us to create and preserve a world civilization, we have in the past permitted two world wars, which within thirty years have brought premature death to seventy million people and have destroyed incalculable spiritual and material assets. Looking at things from every angle, the realists can promise mankind no happy future: the recognizably positive elements, they say, will be incapable of achieving soon enough the necessary transformation of humanity.

'If viewed on purely rational terms,' writes the American social historian Lewis Mumford, 'one might be tempted to accept the dying judgment of H. G. Wells as something more than senile hallucination: "Mind is at the end of its tether". A more benign alternative would call for something like a miracle.'[7]

Political and military motives are no doubt the main explanation for the countless billions spent on space technology and flight to the moon. Such enterprises certainly cannot always be justified by the comparatively limited scientific results they produce.

The fact that expenditure on armaments would one day become too heavy a burden for mankind was foreseen by Bahá'u'lláh a hundred years ago:

'Lay not aside the fear of God, O kings of the earth, and beware that ye transgress not the bounds which the Almighty hath fixed. . . .

'Compose your differences, and reduce your armaments,

that the burden of your expenditures may be lightened, and that your minds and hearts may be tranquillized. Heal the dissensions that divide you, and ye will no longer be in need of any armaments except what the protection of your cities and territories demandeth. . . .

'We have learned that you are increasing your outlay every year, and are laying the burden thereof on your subjects. This, verily, is more than they can bear, and is a grievous injustice. . . .

'If ye pay no heed unto the counsels which, in peerless and unequivocal language, We have revealed in this Tablet, Divine chastisement shall assail you from every direction, and the sentence of His justice shall be pronounced against you. On that day ye shall have no power to resist Him, and shall recognize your own impotence. Have mercy on yourselves and on those beneath you. . . .'[8]

Giving thought to the future of humanity is today no longer the business only of rulers and politicians. To an increasing extent everybody is in duty bound to make his contribution to the shaping of our future.

Science and world peace

In early days, before the sciences had become exact in our modern sense, man's judgments were steeped in myth, superstition and speculative predictions. The development of the exact sciences, therefore, must be considered a historic achievement, which enabled scientists to devote themselves to science only, without regard to the passing events of ordinary life or politics. Anything speculative, including anything to do with the future, they considered to be unscientific and not worth their attention. With the development and use of the atom bomb a radical change has occurred. Since, in the first place, man's understanding of his own situation has lagged behind the practical and technical development of his knowledge, and, moreover, the largely 'value-free' sciences have not contributed to his understanding, even the scientist must now become aware of his responsibility, and concern himself with the non-scientific questions: Where is Man heading? How can his fate be influenced in a positive direction? Repeated pronouncements by scientists show that they are increasingly recognizing their responsibility in this respect. Efforts are even being made, using statistical methods, probability calculations, etc., to start a new science of futurology—if science it can strictly be called—so that, on the strength of it, possible developments in the future may be more or less controlled.

Peace on earth

Bahá'u'lláh said not only that mankind should become one; he also showed how its unity should be brought about. The name Bahá'u'lláh is connected with a 'New Order', of which he testified: 'The world's equilibrium hath been upset through the vibrating influence of this most great, this new World Order. Mankind's ordered life hath been revolutionized through the agency of this unique, this wondrous System—the like of which mortal eyes have never witnessed.'[9]

The Bahá'ís first of all try to establish and prove this New Order of Bahá'u'lláh within their own ranks, so that at the right time it can be applied throughout the world. Bahá'u'lláh also gave a large number of laws and teachings for the improvement of the individual and the community. Many of the ideas of the modern world are already to be found in the writings which he revealed in prison at 'Akká about a hundred years ago. The remarkable encyclical *Pacem in Terris*, for instance, contains no argument that had not been expressed in more comprehensive form by Bahá'u'lláh.[10]

It may be asked what connection there is between a religion and a world order. As understood by the Christian West, religion—at least since the Middle Ages—has been equated with the living faith which helps the *individual* to overcome his sins and achieve salvation.

Now, if we study the New Testament closely and examine especially the passages showing an encounter between Christ, the Jews and the Pharisees, as in the Sermon on the Mount, we observe that Christ always speaks of the heavenly Father, of love and mercy; and at the end of his expositions we read: 'The people were astonished' or 'and they were offended'.[11] Why were they astonished or offended? We must remember that for the Jews strict justice and stern divine law were the essence of religion. In this framework they looked for and found religious experience. Now Jesus had come to them and spoken of love and mercy, no longer 'an eye for an eye, a tooth for a tooth'. Some Jews could not imagine what all this had to do with religion.

In other words, the face of religion changes with the circumstances and needs of the age. For our time Bahá'u'lláh teaches that the redemption of the whole of mankind is more important than the redemption and salvation of the individual. This redemption of mankind and its spiritual unity are what we understand by the establishment of the Kingdom of God 'on earth as it is in heaven'. Since mankind has passed through various stages of unity from the family to the nation, the unity of mankind will not remain an illusion. Yet such unity can be based only on religion, for nothing else appeals so much to the human being in his deepest nature. George Townshend, the well-known churchman and author, says that to 'discard the aid of religion in constructing a new civilization is to reject one of the mightiest instruments of human progress. Down the ages, religion has proved itself a major influence in the integration and remodelling of the social order. The greatest civilizations have been based on the rock of religious faith.'[12] What else could create the spiritual unity of mankind?

The politicians are prisoners of their problems and difficulties. Some of them do not know what they are doing, and others do not know what they *should* do. Today there are two or three Powers, each capable of destroying all human life. In ten years there may be five more, any of them in a position to make this planet uninhabitable. Yesterday Israel sent a rocket into space, today it is Canada, and tomorrow Ethiopia may have atom bombs. The politicians, who are incapable of solving yesterday's problems, are every day plunged into new conflicts. Each new day becomes more dangerous, and everywhere fear is growing. It needs only a failure of nerve on the part of one of the politicians responsible, or even of a subordinate in the armed forces who is entrusted with servicing the automatic weapons and rockets—and disaster is upon us. This fact is so terrifying that most people refuse even to think about it. But assuming that everyone keeps his nerve and nothing happens, what can the politicians do, and how can it go on—how *should* it go on? A lasting peace cannot conceivably be built on mutual fear. It would be nothing but a 'phoney peace'.

Let us start from the premise that mankind, after a long period of division, should become one—not totally uniform, or a 'classless society', but far more, a society of unity in diversity, owing its development to that diversity. The spiritual oneness of mankind, the 'Most Great Peace' as seen by Bahá'u'lláh, is deeply rooted in the civilization of mankind. The prophets have regarded 'peace on earth' as a goal of history. But man has reached a point at which the prophecy about swords being turned into ploughshares must either find its fulfilment in the immediate future or it will never be fulfilled. Our generation could bring about an apocalyptic end. Let no one object that war is in accordance with human nature and therefore inevitable. Men, who have been on this earth for close on two million years, have in a long process of development given up cannibalism.

The unity I have in mind, which represents the central concept of the Bahá'í Faith, cannot be achieved without the fostering of the noblest impulses of the personality. A man must first develop in his inner being a reflection of unity; otherwise he will never conceive the world as one. This future civilization, which will be based on the unity of mankind, is so universal in its range, so splendid in its characteristics, that it cannot be compared to the cultures and civilizations of the past. These great civilizations were like oases scattered through history in time and space, and therefore they could not really make use of and further develop their own and alien cultures of the past. The world civilization to be born, however, will be enriched by a special contribution from every country. Even the less developed nations will create new dimensions for progress and contribute to the world civilization new aspects of creative activity. Much that has been passed over and disregarded till now will be made use of. Much that has been destroyed through unwisdom, prejudice or greed, will come into its own again. The earth's resources, at present unequally distributed, will be shared on a basis of justice with the whole of mankind. The world's economy will be centred, not on Capital or Labour, but in our highest good on this planet: Life itself. In this 'Life Economy' man's education, culture and development will become the main objects of our existence.

Bahá'u'lláh takes full account of this vision of the future, for instance, by making teachers and educators, or corresponding institutions, legatees in a person's estate should he die intestate. In his plan for the law of inheritance the 'spiritual fathers' are given special consideration, that is, those who are concerned with education and culture.

The theory of evolution is of vital importance for the understanding of man and his environment. Foreshadowed by Goethe, enunciated by Darwin, often misused and wrongly interpreted, this theory states that development is an essential part of existence. It took decades to shatter an ossified understanding of creation, which regarded the mere thought of any development as an insult to the Creator. In this battle, alas, the representatives of religion, as so often, were fighting on the wrong side. Yet the actual consequence of this theory of evolution for the human kingdom can only mean that we, the human species, have an undreamt-of development in store for us. Teilhard de Chardin speaks of a great biological event impending. Pierre Bertaux speaks of the human species as being in the process of a mutation; we shall have to get used to this idea, he says, just as without giddiness we have accepted the idea that we are living on a rotating ball. This means on the one hand that we should not see and judge man and his future potentialities merely by the present stage of his development, and on the other hand that our understanding of the Creator's will, determined by this stage in which we find ourselves, is neither final nor exhaustive but merely appropriate at present. In the realm of philosophy and science the idea of the absolute has been overcome; but in the realm of religion most people think they can cling to the old ideas, except for unavoidable concessions imposed by science.

A glorious age lies ahead of us, and with it a world

civilization—provided the present crisis is overcome. In contemplating such an age and such a civilization, however, we must not neglect our immediate tasks. Each one of us must contribute to the establishment of peace, first in his own heart and then for his neighbour. The foundation of the 'Most Great Peace' and the establishment of true unity are the tasks of religious people and idealists, for others cannot change men's hearts and minds. We must not give up and say our numbers are only small. All important changes in human history have come about through the few. Provided we believe, we may be assured that we, following the path of God, are more powerful than anything else in the world. If we do not think in this way, we are materialists. If there were a community which had as its aim the destruction of the whole of humanity, it could not propagate that aim more effectively than by putting into all minds the suggestion: 'But *we* can't do anything!' We must avoid such thoughts. We must fight for a new shape of the world to come. To create the unity of mankind is the greatest work ever undertaken in human history. For it we shall have to expend our strength and muster an idealism unprecedented in the annals of history.

IV

'THE WALLS THAT DIVIDE US DO NOT REACH TO HEAVEN'

The 'Heathen'

NEARLY two thousand years ago Jesus Christ said to his disciples: 'In my Father's house are many mansions . . .'[1] But which of the theologies, Christian or non-Christian, is permeated by the spirit of these words? Up till quite recent times the followers of other religions, that is, the majority of mankind, were all called heathen no matter which camp was considering them. The teachings of other religions were misunderstood and misinterpreted. The Founders of these religions, directly they claimed to be Messengers of God, were dismissed as impostors and false prophets.

A few years ago a little girl in Munich tried to sell me some picture postcards showing Christ on the cross. When I told her that some Christians consider me a heathen, she dropped the cards and ran away. But it is not only simple people who in their religious feeling have turned the 'heathen' into bogeymen. Even a great man like Dante did so; otherwise in his *Divine Comedy* he could scarcely have relegated Muḥammad and 'Alí to the deepest depths of hell. And what is our position today?

Modern religious scholars certainly no longer regard Muḥammad as a liar. Theologians, too, have thoroughly revised the image of him presented throughout centuries of hatred and animosity. This is one of the things which emerged from the declarations of the second Vatican Council. Referring to the civilizations and religions of the missionary countries, Pope John XXIII spoke of 'traces of revealed truth' within them.* But by this token both Christian and non-Christian theology is in the strange position of being able neither to confirm the claims to truth of other religions nor to deny them unconditionally. Consequently, theologians prefer to say nothing.

Rise and development of Islám

In Islám the spirit of tolerance was originally very marked. Jews, Christians and the adherents of Zoroaster were not counted as heathen. When a Muslim married a Christian woman, he was not allowed to stop her going to her church. When she died, she had to be given a Christian burial. If the Christians wanted to build a church, by Muḥammad's instructions the Muslims had to help them with it. He unequivocally impressed on the Arabs the truth of the Messengers of God who had preceded him, and regarded himself as a link in the chain of successive Manifestations. The Qur'án's words are: 'Say ye: "We believe in God, and that which hath been sent down to us, and that which hath been sent down to Abraham and Ismael and Isaac and Jacob and the tribes: and that which hath been given to Moses and to Jesus, and that which was given to the prophets from their Lord. No difference do we make between any of them: and to God are we resigned (Muslims)".'[2] The truth of the Jewish and Christian scriptures is also explicitly confirmed: 'God! there is no god but He, the Living, the Merciful! In truth hath He sent down to thee "the Book," which confirmeth those which precede it: For He had sent down the Law, and the Evangel aforetime, as

* See p. 9.

man's Guidance; and now hath He sent down the "Illumination [Qur'án]".'³

'At the siege of Damascus by the Muslim Arabs, in A.D. 625,' writes the German historian, Peter Bamm, 'the Arab commander Khálid ibn-al-Walíd succeeded in breaking through into the city from the east. When the Damascenes realized this, they spontaneously surrendered the western part of the city to the Arab commander Abú-'Ubaydah, who was encamped on the other side. The Arab commanders met near the Church of Johannes Prodromus.

'For us who have witnessed so much barbarity, what happened sounds almost incredible. The eastern part of the city was regarded as conquered and was looted. The western part was considered to have surrendered and was spared. The Church of John Prodromus in the middle was made accessible to both Muslims and Christians. They entered the sanctuary by the same door. In its eastern part the Muslims prayed to Alláh, in the western part the Christians prayed to the Holy Trinity.'

'The Muslims themselves felt so closely related to the Christian doctrine that a Caliph of Damascus asked an Emperor of Byzantium to hold a joint council with him to establish which was the true doctrine. When I returned from Damascus, I asked one of our most eminent theologians whether God and Alláh were identical. The great man explained to me with a slight smile that this was a question he could not answer off the cuff. I hope to see him again.'⁴ The theologian whom Peter Bamm met will certainly have to consider his answer thoroughly, for all Christians in Arab countries worship Alláh, while their fellow-believers in English-speaking lands glorify God.

Islám had an extremely strong influence on Europe, as shown by historical research, particularly that of the last twenty years. Europe was in most ways overshadowed by Islám for 750 years, nearly as long as the whole period of Graeco–Roman civilization. It was only through Arabic numerals that modern arithmetic became possible. In medicine, astronomy and experimental science, in architecture and philosophy, the Muslims were the teachers of the West. The first European universities and colleges, hospitals, dispensaries and libraries were founded on Islamic models.

In the tenth century the monasteries in the West contained only a few books; and since they were so rare, they were secured by chains. From the ninth to the twelfth century, 95 per cent of the population in Western countries was illiterate. Charlemagne did not try until the last years of his life to master the difficult art of writing; and centuries later the Western aristocracy still took pride in being unable to read or write. Meanwhile in the Islamic countries reading and writing were practically a duty; no Muslim wanted to forego reading the Qur'án for himself. So it is not surprising that a small town like Najaf (in what is now 'Iráq) had a library of 40,000 books; Marághih, a small Persian town, 400,000 books; and Cordobá over a million; while the famous library of the Fáṭimids in Cairo contained 1,600,000 volumes. Private libraries were such a common feature that a doctor invited by the Emir of Bukhára to become his court physician refused simply because he would have needed four hundred camels to transport his library to his new residence. In her book *Allahs Sonne über dem Abendland* [Alláh's Sun over the West] Sigrid Hunke states that the average private library of an educated Muslim of the time contained more books than all the libraries of the West put together.[5] Learned writers in the West even published their books under Arabic names to gain more attention and to ensure they would be taken seriously. The power, charm and greatness of Islamic civilization were so overwhelming that a Crusader from the West wrote home from the East: 'We who were Occidentals have now become Orientals.'

Six hundred years ago the library of the University of Paris medical school owned a single volume, which was the work of a Muslim. To have a copy of this book available for his Court physician, Louis XI was obliged to pay a deposit of twelve marks in silver and one hundred thaler in gold.

No wonder, then, that today there are still two Muslims looking down from the wall of the Paris medical school's main lecture hall: Rhazes [ar-Rází] and Avicenna [Ibn-Síná]. After all, their teachings were completely accepted in Europe for seven hundred years. As long as doctors shut their eyes to the Muslims' medical knowledge, the mediaeval art of healing in Europe followed mystical and mythical paths. It was even feared that the use of secular remedies to make people recover might endanger the good of their souls. In any case, however, treatment had to be preceded by a confession. At the Lateran Council of 1215, Pope Innocent III issued a decree forbidding any doctor to treat a patient who had not been to confession first. Anyone who violated this decree was expelled from the Church. Those who let themselves be treated by a non-Christian doctor were excommunicated. The Council declared surgery to be a dishonourable trade, and its practice was not to be allowed.[6]

The Muslims, however, developed a medical school surpassing anything that had gone before. Karl Sudhoff, one of the first to produce a scientific history of medicine, saw Avicenna's work as an achievement unique in the medical literature of all time. The Muslims also elevated the practice of surgery to the rank of a science and developed a professional code for the physician, stating that he should 'give treatment to his enemies in the same spirit, with the same compassion and readiness with which he treats those he loves.'⁷

The hospital in Strasbourg was the first in Europe to have a doctor on its established staff. The one in Leipzig followed suit in 1517, the Hôtel Dieu in Paris in 1536. Eight hundred years earlier the Caliph al-Walíd had founded the first Arab hospital and appointed some doctors to it. There were then 860 doctors living in Baghdád alone, not counting the medical officers employed by the government—at a time, that is, when there was not a single doctor to be found along the entire middle reaches of the Rhine. We should bear in mind that in 1209 the Paris synod still forbade the monks to read writings on natural science. The study of such books was declared a sin.*

Muḥammad's attitude to the sciences was quite different. He recommended everyone to strive to acquire knowledge, even if he had to travel as far as China for the purpose. The Qur'án contains this significant question: 'Shall they who have knowledge and they who have it not, be treated alike?'⁹ Physics and chemistry owe many fundamental hypotheses to Muslim scholars. The Muslims created the method of systematic observation: they could reproduce at will the results of their investigations, so that they were capable at any time of furnishing scientific evidence for their findings. According to an assessment by the English historian Custom, they developed experimental chemistry to such a point that 'the discoveries of modern organic and inorganic chemistry were necessary to bring it once more to the level to which it had been lifted by the Arabs.'¹⁰

---

* There was always a school of thought in Christendom which regarded the study of nature and its laws as unimportant and unworthy of man's destiny. It was in this spirit that Thomas Aquinas wrote: 'The slightest insight anyone may gain into the most sublime things is more desirable than the most assured knowledge of lowly things.'⁸

Again, if we look at the question of language, how did it happen that Aramaic, the language of Christ, gave way for ever to the language of Muḥammad? How could it happen that within decades the language of a tribe developed into the world language of its time? How could it happen that individual tribes warring among themselves, who had hardly ever had any cultural or political importance, created within a very short time a civilization which was for centuries a guiding light to the world? These are some of the questions which Sigrid Hunke has justifiably asked.

Most scholars agree that these almost miraculous events would have been unthinkable without the impulse of Muḥammad. Much injustice has been done in Europe to Muḥammad's words and deeds. While Europeans have always managed to make a distinction between Christ's teaching and the un-Christian actions of his 'followers' throughout history, they have held Muḥammad responsible for all the wrongs Muslims have committed over the centuries in the name of religion. But as evidence of the tolerance, generosity and spiritual attitude of the founder of Islám, we may look at the treaties later concluded by the Muslims according to his example.

The peace treaty with the city of Jerusalem concluded by ʿUmar, the second caliph, reads: 'This treaty is valid for all Christian subjects, priests, monks and nuns. It guarantees them security and protection whoever they are. We as the Caliph are in duty bound to ensure protection for Ourselves, Our followers and all Christian subjects who fulfil their obligations. Their [Christian] churches, houses and their places of pilgrimage are assured of appropriate protection, and so are those who frequent these places: the Georgians, Abyssinians, Jacobites, Nestorians and all those recognizing the Prophet Jesus. All these deserve consideration, since they have been honoured before by a document from the Prophet Muḥammad, to which he put his seal and in which he asked Us explicitly to be kind to them and to grant them protection. Therefore We as the Head of all true believers are required to show Our kindness, and this as a sign of Our devotion to him, who has already shown you his kindness and mercy. Accordingly, as pilgrims in all the countries of Islám, at sea and on land, they are exempted from payment of all duties and taxes and from the poll-tax. When they enter the Church of the Holy Sepulchre, and throughout their pilgrimage, no kind of tax is to be levied from them.... Whoever has read this treaty and violates it between today and the day of the Last Judgment or who deals with them contrary to this treaty, breaks the Covenant of Alláh and that of His beloved Prophet...'[11]

'They are just,' wrote the Patriarch of Jerusalem to the Patriarch of Constantinople in the ninth century, 'and do unto us no injustice or any outrages. They grant those of different faith in their realm all religious and civic liberties—as long as they pay their poll-tax and obey their masters.'[12]

The French historian Seignobos writes: 'Let us examine the two civilizations which, in the eleventh century, divided between them the ancient world. In the West miserable little towns, peasants' huts and uncomfortable fortresses, a country always troubled by war where one could not travel ten leagues without running the risk of being set upon; in the East, Constantinople, Cairo, Damascus, Baghdád ... with their marble palaces, their workshops, their schools, their bazaars, their gardens which covered several acres, a well-watered countryside spread with villages and the incessant movement of merchants who travelled peacefully from Spain to Persia. There is no doubt that the Musulman and Byzantine worlds were richer, better policed, better lit than the western world. The Christians felt their own culture to be inferior, they admired wonderingly the marvels of the East, and those who wished to educate themselves went to the Arab schools.

'In the eleventh century, these two worlds began to know something of each other; the barbarous Christians went amongst the civilized Musulmans in two ways: through war and through trade.'[13]

The decline of Islám

But over the centuries the situation changed. The Muslims, who once held a leading position intellectually and materially, and were the standard-bearers of science and education, are today more than 80 per cent illiterate. The Islamic countries which at first made incomparable contributions to the development of culture and civilization, must at present start again as 'developing countries'. Their generous tolerance of spirit also fell by the wayside. To protect the young seed of belief in God from barbarian tribes, Muḥammad had authorized 'Holy War': 'And fight for the cause of God against those who fight against you: but commit not the injustice of attacking them first . . .', it says in the Qur'án.[14] But in the course of time the bounds were exceeded repeatedly. A state was even reached where the feuds and wars of power politics within the Islamic world were declared to be 'Holy Wars'.

The long and sad story of Islám's decline cannot be told in a few words. What is evident is that Islám was no more capable than Christianity of creating a lasting basis for tolerance, love, unity and peace.

The seeds of understanding

Where are the impulses today, then, for a universal

understanding? Dare we hope in our age to create on the foundation of religion a spiritual *entente* common to all men, races and nations, containing the embryo of the world civilization to come? Will the Bahá'í Faith succeed in winning men over to the spiritual unity it teaches? Will Bahá'u'lláh be able to complete the work of Christ and the work of Muḥammad? History will one day testify whether the Bahá'í Faith succeeded in reaching the goal it set itself. Undoubtedly, through Bahá'u'lláh new forces have been released which increasingly are working all over the world towards the ideal of unity.

Some of these forces will lead to a settlement between the various races, others will bring reconciliation and unification in the political field, from a 'United Europe' to the 'United Nations'. Others again will create the conditions for a comprehensive unity in the economic field. All efforts for economic union, even aid to developing countries, derive from the basic idea of unity. In the field of cultural exchange, in attempts to introduce a universal auxiliary language and universal script (such as Esperanto), we find people consciously or unconsciously working towards a universal unity. In all kinds of religious denominations, Christian and non-Christian, we find moves towards lifting the barriers and opening the doors in the religious field. The Bahá'í Faith sees as its task the provision of that spiritual centre for all these efforts towards unity and peace, without which they have no chance of surviving the crises of the day and attaining long-term success. Perhaps our generation will witness the development forecast by a Protestant clergyman with whom Marcus Bach exchanged ideas and whom he quotes as follows: 'If these Bahá'ís ever get going, they may take the country by storm!'[15]

Many critics ask: What is so new in the Bahá'í Faith?

In fact, a great deal is new: the comprehensive idea of a world order,* and many commandments and principles were for the first time in religious and spiritual history enunciated by Bahá'u'lláh.

But this question is not really so important. It is the healing power of a medicine that matters, not whether its ingredients are known or unknown. If you look more closely at any of the historic religions, much that appears new at first sight turns out to have parallels in earlier testimonies. Expressed in words, the teachings of all Holy Scriptures seem slight enough. Thus Buddha taught: Learn to control your passions, revere life and all living things, and try to liberate yourself from the perpetual cycle of birth and death. Zoroaster's teaching can be summed up in the words: Strive for good words, good works and good thoughts. Krishna commanded: Be virtuous, try to see yourself as a part of the whole and to attune your energy to the forces of nature; do not let habits and appearances keep you from penetrating to the reality behind them. The message of Jesus was: Love your heavenly Father and your neighbour; be pure in your intentions and actions, and do not let yourself be seduced by possessions and power; then you will attain

* Shoghi Effendi has written: 'The Bahá'í Commonwealth of the future, of which this vast Administrative Order is the sole framework, is, both in theory and practice, not only unique in the entire history of political institutions, but can find no parallel in the annals of any of the world's recognized religious systems. No form of democratic government; no system of autocracy or of dictatorship, whether monarchical or republican; no intermediary scheme of a purely aristocratic order; nor even any of the recognized types of theocracy, whether it be the Hebrew Commonwealth, or the various Christian ecclesiastical organizations, or the Imamate or the Caliphate in Islám—none of these can be identified or be said to conform with the Administrative Order which the master-hand of its perfect Architect has fashioned.'

'Let no one, while this System is still in its infancy, misconceive its character, belittle its significance or misrepresent its purpose.'[16]

the kingdom of heaven. Muḥammad preached: Worship only the one God, keep the divine commandments, and you will be granted eternal happiness.

As Lewis Mumford puts it: 'Plainly the precepts and doctrines of axial religions* are not by themselves sufficient to account for the dynamics of their appeal—or the positive transformations that issue from it.'[17] This positive transforming force, which is impenetrable by scientific means, is called by the Bahá'ís the creative Word of God: 'Let there be light: and there was light.'[18]

Bahá'u'lláh writes: 'Is it within human power ... to effect in the constituent elements of any of the minute and indivisible particles of matter so complete a transformation as to transmute it into purest gold? Perplexing and difficult as this may appear, the still greater task of converting satanic strength into heavenly power is one that We have been empowered to accomplish. The Force capable of such a transformation transcendeth the potency of the Elixir itself. The Word of God, alone, can claim the distinction of being endowed with the capacity required for so great and far-reaching a change.'[19]

The Bahá'í Faith in the light of critical analysis

The respect in which the Bahá'ís hold the Founders and Holy Scriptures of other religions has prompted some superficial observers to state that the Bahá'í Faith is a syncretic religion, taking over various ideas from other religions and making these into an artificial unity. This statement is historically incorrect and unfounded in substance.

Had the Founder of the Bahá'í Faith been active in a country where different religions and philosophies came into

* The universal religions, such as Buddhism, Zoroastrianism, Christianity and Islám.

close contact with each other and a synthesis in the form of a syncretic religion was conceivable, there might possibly have seemed to be some historical truth in the charge. But Bahá'u'lláh appeared in Persia, a country where at the time over 98 per cent of the population was Muslim and there were hardly any points of contact with other religions, Indian or European. Moreover, Bahá'u'lláh, like other Manifestations of God, had never attended a school. He spent no less than forty years of his life isolated in prison or exile.

The assertion that his message is syncretic is unfounded in substance because he never made a compromise. He did not teach that what the Jews or the various Islamic or Christian denominations or sects said, was true. What he did teach was that Moses, Krishna, Zoroaster, Buddha, Christ and Muḥammad were Messengers of God speaking to men at God's command. But men, by their interpretations and speculations, narrowed and darkened the horizon of religion and distorted the divine word. To change the metaphor, theologies, dogmas and interpretations ossified the living religion, until it splintered into hundreds of different schools. These religious systems split up within themselves and also became more and more estranged from the other religions, until every sect and denomination claimed absolute truth for its own tenets and dogmas.

Bahá'u'lláh's teaching is not syncretic. He does not make an appeal to the theologians of the different religions to tolerate each other and meet each other halfway on particular questions. What he does say is that people should once and for all give up challenging the living Word of God with their own opinions. This is why in Bahá'í worship the sermon no longer has relevance. In Bahá'í Houses of Worship the Holy Scriptures must not be interpreted by the word of man.

Bahá'u'lláh desires that man in his encounter with God's sacred Word should free himself from his own conceits and ideas. For truth is not something we can take into our possession. We must cleanse our hearts as we would a mirror so that the Sun of Truth can shine within them. On this point 'Abdu'l-Bahá, the Centre of Bahá'u'lláh's Covenant,* says in his mild and kindly language: 'We must not look for truth in the deeds and actions of nations; we must investigate truth at its divine source and summon all mankind to unity in the reality itself.'[20]

It is not necessary to degrade Muḥammad in order to exalt Christ. It is not necessary to decry Zoroaster in order to prove our love for Moses. Every one of God's Manifestations whom we refuse to recognize will judge us in the words which Christ addressed to the Pharisees: 'For had ye believed Moses, ye would have believed me . . .'[21]

This spiritual attitude of the Bahá'ís prompted Arnold Toynbee to refer to the Bahá'í Faith as the most tolerant of the Judaic religions.[22]

Bahá'u'lláh's teachings have been criticized as rationalistic, appealing only to man's reason. In this connection people quote—as if it were a drawback—various principles of his teachings likely to appeal to modern consciousness, such as the harmony between religion and science, the need for religious unity, the overcoming of all prejudices, and the independent search for truth. The objection is raised that these doctrines are essentially a philosophy and have no direct connection with religion. Such an appraisal can be made, however, only through a superficial knowledge of the Bahá'í Faith. Admittedly in expounding and defending their faith the Bahá'ís must consider everything which in an enlightened age concerns man intellectually. But to refute

* See p. 17.

the charge of rationalism it is only necessary to read extracts from Bahá'u'lláh's mystical writings, like *The Seven Valleys* or *The Hidden Words*, to find other features of this young Faith. But the really essential point in the Bahá'í message is that God has revealed Himself again in our age in the person of Bahá'u'lláh. He is the perfect teacher of mankind, the perfect physician for man's ailments, and without him man has no chance of surviving. His authority is the divine authority, and he is the true law-giver.

As he himself testifies: 'Know verily that the essence of justice and the source thereof are both embodied in the ordinances prescribed by Him who is the Manifestation of the Self of God amongst men ... He doth verily incarnate the highest, the infallible standard of justice unto all creation. Were His law to be such as to strike terror into the hearts of all that are in heaven and on earth, that law is naught but manifest justice. The fears and agitation which the revelation of this law provokes in men's hearts should indeed be likened to the cries of the suckling babe weaned from his mother's milk ... Were men to discover the motivating purpose of God's Revelation, they would assuredly cast away their fears, and, with hearts filled with gratitude, rejoice with exceeding gladness.'[23]

It has sometimes been said that the Bahá'í Faith is a sect of Islám. But such a mistake is less common these days, as the nature of the Bahá'í Faith has now been more thoroughly investigated. Even so, the following statement in the verdict of 10 May 1925 by the Islamic Court of Appeal of Beba (Egypt), cited by Shoghi Effendi, may serve to clarify matters: 'The Bahá'í Faith is a new religion, entirely independent, with beliefs, principles and laws of its own, which differ from, and are utterly in conflict with, the beliefs, principles and laws of Islám. No Bahá'í, therefore, can be regarded a Muslim or vice versa, even as no Buddhist, Brahmin, or Christian can be regarded a Muslim or vice versa.'[24]

In 1961 an expert on comparative religions, Professor von Glasenapp of Tübingen University, wrote of the Bahá'í Faith: 'The religion of the Bahá'ís, although derived from Islám, represents an independent form of faith, not an Islamic sect. Otherwise, by the same token, we should have to consider Christianity a Jewish sect, since it derived from Judaism. As I have pointed out in my book *Die nichtchristlichen Religionen*,* the Bahá'í Faith claims to be a new world religion including and going beyond all preceding forms of faith.'[25]

Excessive optimism is another charge made against the Bahá'ís, especially by Christians. They are said to be enthusiastic dreamers, who do not want to recognize the bad in people. They talk about peace, about the oneness of mankind, a new world order, and the unity of religions. They strive for the introduction of a universal language and script, and dream of a culture and civilization for all mankind; whereas, the fact is, man is burdened with original sin, and Satan is at work as never before. On closer observation it is seen that the attitude of the Bahá'ís is not at all unrealistic. They are concerned with the condition and needs of the time probably more than any other community.

What could we expect if believers were to give up their hopes of unity and peace? Are not our technological advances and potentialities in themselves evidence that the long-desired time of universal unity is irrevocably drawing nearer?

Since it is precisely the religious leaders who refuse to recognize the spiritual unity of mankind as the central

* *The Non-Christian Religions*. (Published in German by Fischer, 1957.)

spiritual and religious factor in our era, I would remind them above all that nearly two thousand years ago Jesus Christ taught the prayer: 'Thy kingdom come, Thy will be done . . .' Referring to this, 'Abdu'l-Bahá is reported as saying, 'Do you think he would have told you to pray for something that will never come?'

Finally, the Bahá'ís are accused of making truth relative. Just as in a department store a selection of all kinds of goods is offered, so, it is said, a great variety of ideas can be picked up from the Bahá'í Faith, according to one's viewpoint, but not the single and absolute truth. This charge is based on a misunderstanding of the nature of religion.

According to Bahá'u'lláh, the Messenger of God is endowed with absolute authority, sitting on the throne of 'He . . . doeth whatsoever He willeth'.[26] Consistent with the needs and receptivity of the people of a particular age, God's revelation to man is relative, for man possesses no capacity to recognize and sustain absolute truth. For Bahá'u'lláh's followers it would be intolerable, as he states, 'to believe that all revelation is ended, that the portals of Divine mercy are closed, that from the daysprings of eternal holiness no sun shall rise again, that the ocean of everlasting bounty is forever stilled, and that out of the tabernacle of ancient glory the Messengers of God have ceased to be made manifest . . .'[27]

It would be presumptuous to believe that absolute truth could be conclusively captured, formulated or, much less, its meaning exhausted by the inadequate, time-conditioned, ever-changing and evolving language of men.

The theologians of the Middle Ages and of modern times have been guilty of such presumption, in maintaining that the earth—a place where the Son of God dwelt, and where his representative the Pope resides—must be absolutely static, since otherwise the celestial and earthly order would cease to exist.

Bahá'u'lláh's postulate of the unity of the Revealers means that people have always been brothers and sisters, but they have not realized it. It means that God's plan of redemption is more comprehensive than we have hitherto assumed. We cannot solve the problem merely by professing our will to be good Buddhists, good Jews or good Christians and acting as such. For it is only through Bahá'u'lláh that we can clear the way back to Buddha, Moses or Christ and learn to understand their meaning for our own day.

Bahá'u'lláh's message offers those who follow him the certainty that by his advent the whole of mankind has once again been immersed in the sea of forgiveness and purification. Thus today the whole of mankind must be considered God's chosen people.

We should do well to remember the famous saying of the Ṣúfís (Islamic mystics): 'There are as many ways to God as there are men.' We should do well also to ponder Christ's words again and again: 'In my Father's house are many mansions: if it were not so, I would have told you. I go to prepare a place for you.'[28] The new Revelation of God, so it seems to us Bahá'ís, has signposted the way to the 'many mansions'.

V

THE NEW EARTH

'Through the movement of Our Pen of glory We have, at the bidding of the omnipotent Ordainer, breathed a new life into every human frame, and instilled into every word a fresh potency. All created things proclaim the evidences of this world-wide regeneration. This is the most great, the most joyful tidings imparted by the pen of this wronged One to mankind.'[1]

Bahá'u'lláh

Man's progress towards unity

IN Persia, as no doubt in most other countries, history as a subject taught in schools was more or less the history of wars. A king who had fought no wars during his reign was considered insignificant, while one who had fought and conquered many peoples was an important monarch. This applied outside the class-rooms as well; the whole of political philosophy, until very recent times, was based on the idea that war was something inevitable, was in fact the father of all things.

The Bahá'ís see history in a different light: as a development towards unity at progressively higher levels. In the course of time men have created the unity of the family, the clan, the people and the nation; now they must start bringing to fruition the unity of all mankind. Vital impulses towards the realization of each level of unity have been given by the Messengers of God, the founders of religions. Adam, for instance, may be considered a symbol of the unity of the human personality, since through him man became conscious of his free will. Abraham was the founder of a clan, Moses welded the tribes of Israel into a united people. It is interesting to study the Old Testament from the viewpoint of God's guidance to mankind for the achievement of these higher levels of unity in each case. Muḥammad created the nation in its modern sense. His followers, of different origins, races and peoples—from the Ganges to the Pyrenees—were equal before the law.

It is man's task today to bring together into unity all the inhabitants of the earth, regardless of their country or the colour of their skin. Is it justifiable to hold such optimistic ideas about the future of mankind? There is no doubt that each successive level of unity was realized in earlier times. To find out whether the conditions and needs of our age will allow and enforce universal unity, or work against it, we must take a closer look at what distinguishes our age from the past.

Science and technology are changing the world

In terms of space the countries of the world have obviously moved closer together. Technology, as Toynbee says, has 'annihilated' distance. Consequently, a country cannot live in isolation, as it still could in our forefathers' time. Moreover, a country's fate today depends not only on its leaders' decisions. In general we can say that the fates of all the different countries are interwoven. The ideas of powerful men in Washington, Moscow or Peking influence individuals and peoples everywhere. We are living today in a world which is not only rapidly developing, but in which the pace of progress is accelerating. A glance at the history of mankind should make this clear.

Two million years may have elapsed between the time when man first used a stone as a tool and the time when he deliberately made a tool out of a stone. From stonemason to blacksmith took 50,000 years, from blacksmith to steam engine 5,000 years, from locomotive to space-travel 150 years. Similarly, in the field of literature fewer books were written from the time script was invented until the beginning of the Second World War than have been published since then.

The accelerated rate of progress, as Lewis Mumford shows, is like the graph of an exponential function. Our consciousness cannot yet absorb and digest the magnitude of this development. At the beginning of the fifties, it was said that human discoveries in various spheres had doubled within a century (from 1850 to 1950). Now we hear that it took only another fifteen years (from 1950 to 1965) for such knowledge to double again. Neither scientists nor philosophers, nor even theologians, can explain this sudden and unexpected unfoldment of science and technology, or, as the historian Hermann Glaser puts it, 'how after a thousand years of stagnation technological development has turned all at once into a raging torrent'.[2]

Yet it is becoming more and more apparent that there is nothing fortuitous about such development. Rather, there are striking signs that it is part of a purposive and meaningful process which favours and even compels the unity of mankind, universal justice and world-wide peace.* Galileo recognized that nature has been 'written in a mathematical language', and men of research have always been exhilarated by the experience that nature answers them if addressed in its own language, a language which man is learning to master with more and more confidence. (Many sciences, however—biochemistry, medicine, psychology and new

* For the Bahá'í ideas on this development and its causes, compare pp. 34–6.

branches of physics, to name only a few—are still in the early stages of their development.) Thus the presumed limits of man's physical and intellectual possibilities have had to be continually revised. To illustrate this, we might recall that when railways first came in, there were scientists who maintained in all seriousness that a speed of twenty miles an hour was dangerous and excessive, not only for men but also for animals. Today, a few generations later, hardly anyone expresses qualms about men travelling through space for weeks at a speed of 20,000 miles an hour.

While man changes the world, he changes himself, and the limits to such change are nowhere nearly in sight. Science and technology today have opened up to everyone possibilities which were closed before, even to emperor and king. Wide areas of our freedom are continually disappearing, it is true, and things we could once decide freely for ourselves are now things we cannot avoid doing—or having done to us. On the other hand, new horizons of freedom are appearing just as constantly. It is not only man's powers over his environment which are being extended by science and technology, but also his field of intellectual activity, provided he remains master of his inventions and can absorb satisfactorily the new developments.

Meanwhile, our understanding of time has also undergone a fundamental change. Owing to Einstein's theory of relativity it has ceased to be an absolute dimension. Every particle in the whole universe has its own time, which, moreover, can be extended or curtailed by alteration in its speed (there is no particle without speed). Again, time and space are so interconnected that one dimension is non-existent without the other. The concept of infinite divisibility of time and space has also been destroyed by the quantum theory. Matter and time are not infinitely divisible. Even though these discoveries may have very little practical significance for our daily life, they are still calculated to rob us of our illusions of the 'absolute' in nature and its phenomena. Man is recognizing more and more that he cannot regard himself as the measure of all things and the centre of the universe.

This realization is strengthened by the belief of many scientists that ours is not the only inhabited planet, nor our form of intelligence the only possible form. The well-known astronomer Fred Hoyle has reckoned that in our Milky Way there are probably between a hundred thousand and a million planets which have similar conditions of life to those on earth. Applying this figure to the whole universe, we arrive at a figure of a hundred thousand billion inhabited planets. Similar calculations were broadcast on Radio Moscow in September 1959 by the Soviet astronomer Felix Segals.

Many modern biochemists go a step further, saying that the conditions necessary for life are latent in matter. This would mean, in the language of the 'materialists', that all living things are a natural further development and new form of expression of 'matter'; in the language of believers, that there is no such thing as dead matter. Everything that exists is by its origins equipped with the potential of being awakened to life. Although the Protestant and Catholic Churches do not exclude the possibility of life existing on other planets, they refuse from the outset to accept such a fact as a basis for discussing the claim to uniqueness in the historical mission of Jesus Christ—although this was an event on our planet.

As mankind goes on developing, we find the density of the earth's population increasing proportionately. Within two hundred generations it has increased a hundredfold. By the year 2000, which many of our generation will live to see, we must expect that the present numbers will have doubled. As a consequence of this 'population explosion' on the one hand, and the great scientific and technological advances on the other, we find an even greater increase in the communication media—books, newspapers, journals, radio, television. These create a link between individuals by which the desires, thoughts and actions of each one of us are influenced and shaped to an unprecedented degree. The 'planetization of mankind', in Teilhard de Chardin's phrase, takes such an inevitable course that no individuals, groups or religious communities have the power to withstand it.

This means that tomorrow's men and women will be fundamentally different from yesterday's. We may hope that such world-wide communication will make it impossible for mankind to base its feelings on primitive friend-or-foe categories. The inhabitants of towns about fifteen miles apart could once regard each other collectively as enemies. Only a hundred years ago individual German peoples and states were fighting among themselves. Today it is already difficult to influence Europeans in such a way that various states think of the others collectively as enemies. So far as we can form a picture of 'homo progressivus', as de Chardin calls the new human type, he will have the essential characteristic that even antagonism between different members of the species will bind them to each other. One is tempted to say that there is a particular dimension of life where every effort, in whichever direction, can only lead to a *rapprochement*.

I have already mentioned that there is a discrepancy between our thoughts, feelings and actions on the one hand and the most recent state of knowledge in the field of science and technology on the other. Our consciousness is not so constituted as to absorb immediately the achievements and discoveries of science; and the time-lag of years, decades or even generations, represents a danger of the first order for mankind. That is why it is one of the most vital tasks of education to make young people, in particular, familiar with this idea. For to realize the discrepancy between the facts and our response to them means to reduce their dangers. Technology, which has created the new conditions, not only gives us freedom but new fetters as well. It makes us independent by loosening the bonds of space and time, revealing to us new and far wider potentialities; but it also uproots man and makes him a stranger to himself. It is particularly in crisis situations, such as rail strikes, sudden gas, water or electricity breakdowns, that we realize how far we have forfeited our material independence and come to rely on technology.

These developments have imposed on us a responsibility which we can no longer carry out unaided or through existing institutions. The steam engine could still be curbed by a strong arm; electricity is being controlled by public corporations. There should be an international authority for the atom, but no such authority exists—one reason why we cannot live without anxiety. But at least owing to the facts of technology the world has reluctantly arrived at a modicum of unity; although at present it is mostly a unity in misfortune. When a war breaks out in Korea or Vietnam, when there is tension in the Middle East or in Cuba, or a cold war is waged over Berlin, the whole of mankind has to suffer from it. Because of the conditions of our age, every serious conflict assumes an international character.

During the past hundred years intensive efforts have been going on to control nature. Now we should at last set about trying to control technology for the benefit of humanity, realizing that man can no longer afford to disregard universal unity—implying unity in both space and time. Not only the different races, nations and religious communities, which have been kept apart by geography, but also people at different stages of development, with their varying cultures and mentalities—the so-called civilized countries, countries under feudal régimes, and primitive races—must come together under the 'shade of one tree'. The State of Israel is a small experiment on these lines, for in that country people at various stages of development have converged from all corners of the world. They are all trying to create a truly united country, and it looks as if their attempt may succeed.

Today 70 per cent of mankind are in the 'developing countries'. Over 60 per cent live below subsistence level and cannot rely on obtaining the necessities of life; and 66 per cent can neither read nor write. This means that a majority of human beings scarcely ever have the opportunity of exercising their free will and reason or of realizing their latent talents and potentialities which must just go to waste. The great technological advances are so far confined to a few countries, and most of the earth's inhabitants never get beyond a child's level in their intellectual development. But the civilized countries, too, have essentially developed only in material respects. That is why even in the most advanced countries only a tiny minority is concerned with spiritual questions and problems; everyone else is solely concerned with progress in the material field. In America the point has already been reached where 96 per cent of all work is done by machines; another 2 per cent is done by animals, and only the remaining 2 per cent is reserved for man; thus everybody in America has forty-nine servants, 'technological slaves', working for his benefit. And this figure will go up a good deal further.

Man has indeed fully exploited God's command in the Old Testament to 'subdue' the earth. He is also told in Genesis to give things names, and thus he defines and makes them useful to himself.[3] Technological progress in our age has been so great that it conditions our whole consciousness. Should we hear, for instance, that a car had been produced to drive on land, in the air, on and under water, we should accept it. On 1 April a few years ago orders came in from several firms when a shirt factory offered as a joke a shirt which would not get dirty through use. There are scarcely any limits we can imagine to the possibilities of technological progress, and indeed this progress will go on changing our world and our views of the world more and more in the immediate future. In former generations man only needed to make small adjustments to his picture of the world; today every generation must come to terms with a new picture.

God's statement in the Old Testament, 'let them have dominion over . . . all the earth',[4] has been amplified by Bahá'u'lláh: 'All that is in heaven and earth I have ordained for thee, except the human heart, which I have made the habitation of My beauty and glory . . .'[5]

The process of creation is not yet finished. The ancient Greeks had already discovered that everything is continually in a state of flux. And the Bahá'í Faith does not recognize static conditions even for the hereafter. In God's infinite worlds to come the human spirit will make progress by divine grace. Thus in the widest sense we are in a field of relativity. In our nuclear age we are aware of the extent of this relativity. For religion this means that true faith cannot be defined exhaustively by formulas and dogmas. The Word of God is, and will remain, the balance by which truth is weighed, its basis and standard.

The advances, crises, changes and trials of our time are so immense that it is essential for religion and science to work hand in hand. This is one of the most important demands our age makes of us, the only way in which the integrity of the human spirit can be preserved. Critical reason offers a guarantee that piety does not degenerate into superstition, and faith prevents science from losing control and encouraging materialism. The Bahá'í Faith insists that religion must be rational in its outlook. Considering that the hundreds of pseudo-religions and ideologies which exist today all recognize the claims of reason, so much the less can the truly religious afford to deny the harmony between faith and reason, two aspects of one truth—for there is only *one* truth.

A new era

The Bahá'ís believe that through Bahá'u'lláh mankind has entered a new era, which cannot be compared with any past era. We are making a completely fresh start, from a new 'Year Nought', which draws a sharp dividing line between yesterday and today. We have the privilege of living in such a period, but it is hard to grasp this truth. To help us understand, let us begin with the idea that matter is a reflection of spirit. Then let us look at the scientific and technological potential of mankind today and see how much our century differs from all preceding ones, for worse as well as for better. In the armouries of the world there are so many weapons of destruction waiting to be used that their explosive power would be enough to cover the entire surface of the earth with 3.5 mm of dynamite, over a million times as much as existed a hundred years ago. The Bahá'ís believe there is a spiritual cause for this development.

Referring to our age, 'Abdu'l-Bahá said: 'So loud is the call that reverberates from the Abhá Kingdom* that mortal ears are well-nigh deafened with its vibrations. The whole creation, methinks, is being disrupted and is bursting asunder through the shattering influence of the Divine summons issued from the throne of glory. More than this I cannot write.'[6]

To mark the importance of our age as against the past, Bahá'u'lláh in *The Book of Certitude*† quotes an Islamic tradition according to which all human knowledge, symbolically speaking, consists of twenty-seven letters. Until the coming of the Báb, (who, as herald and forerunner of Bahá'u'lláh, introduced a new cycle in the history of religion and mankind), men possessed only two letters. The remaining twenty-five letters are being added in this new era.[7] With two letters few words can be written, but with twenty-seven an infinite number. Such a future, infinitely rich and beautiful in its potentialities, caused the Founder of the Bahá'í Faith to make the solemn declaration: 'I testify before God to the greatness, the inconceivable greatness of this Revelation'.[8]

'We have caused every soul to expire,' he testifies in another passage, 'by virtue of Our irresistible and all-subduing sovereignty. We have, then, called into being a new creation, as a token of Our grace unto men.'[9]

If we admit that the world of today is totally different from the world in which Jesus Christ preached two thousand years ago, then the commands and teachings of the new revelation must take into account this difference. Love of one's neighbour, the central point in Christ's teaching,

---

* Literally, the 'Most Glorious Kingdom'. A Bahá'í term referring to the eternal spiritual kingdom.
† *Kitáb-i-Íqán.*

has been amplified by Bahá'u'lláh. The individual is no more, but also no less, than a cell in the body of all mankind. Bahá'u'lláh teaches that humanity, as well as individual man, has in accordance with God's will been created in organic unity after His own image.

Of this organic world community Shoghi Effendi writes: 'The unity of the human race, as envisaged by Bahá'u'lláh, implies the establishment of a world commonwealth in which all nations, races, creeds and classes are closely and permanently united, and in which the autonomy of its state members and the personal freedom and initiative of the individuals that compose them are definitely and completely safeguarded. This commonwealth must, as far as we can visualize it, consist of a world legislature, whose members will, as the trustees of the whole of mankind, ultimately control the entire resources of all the component nations, and will enact such laws as shall be required to regulate the life, satisfy the needs and adjust the relationships of all races and peoples. A world executive, backed by an international Force, will carry out the decisions arrived at, and apply the laws enacted by, this world legislature, and will safeguard the organic unity of the whole commonwealth. A world tribunal will adjudicate and deliver its compulsory and final verdict in all and any disputes that may arise between the various elements constituting this universal system. A mechanism of world inter-communication will be devised, embracing the whole planet, freed from national hindrances and restrictions, and functioning with marvellous swiftness and perfect regularity. A world metropolis will act as the nerve centre of a world civilization, the focus towards which the unifying forces of life will converge and from which its energizing influences will radiate. A world language will either be invented or chosen from among the existing languages and will be taught in the schools of all the federated nations as an auxiliary to their mother tongue. A world script, a world literature, a uniform and universal system of currency, of weights and measures, will simplify and facilitate intercourse and understanding among the nations and races of mankind. In such a world society, science and religion, the two most potent forces in human life, will be reconciled, will co-operate, and will harmoniously develop. The press will, under such a system, while giving full scope to the expression of the diversified views and convictions of mankind, cease to be mischievously manipulated by vested interests, whether private or public, and will be liberated from the influence of contending governments and peoples. The economic resources of the world will be organized, its sources of raw materials will be tapped and fully utilized, its markets will be co-ordinated and developed, and the distribution of its products will be equitably regulated.

'National rivalries, hatreds, and intrigues will cease, and racial animosity and prejudice will be replaced by racial amity, understanding and co-operation. The causes of religious strife will be permanently removed, economic barriers and restrictions will be completely abolished, and the inordinate distinction between classes will be obliterated. Destitution on the one hand, and gross accumulation of ownership on the other, will disappear. The enormous energy dissipated and wasted on war, whether economic or political, will be consecrated to such ends as will extend the range of human inventions and technical development, to the increase of the productivity of mankind, to the extermination of disease, to the extension of scientific research, to the raising of the standard of physical health, to the sharpening and refinement of the human brain, to the exploitation of the unused and unsuspected resources of the planet, to the prolongation of human life, and to the furtherance of any other agency that can stimulate the intellectual, the moral, and spiritual life of the entire human race.

'A world federal system, ruling the whole earth and exercising unchallengeable authority over its unimaginably vast resources, blending and embodying the ideals of both the East and the West, liberated from the curse of war and its miseries, and bent on the exploitation of all the available sources of energy on the surface of the planet, a system in which Force is made the servant of Justice, whose life is sustained by its universal recognition of one God and by its allegiance to one common Revelation—such is the goal towards which humanity, impelled by the unifying forces of life, is moving.'[10]

VI

THE HERALD

*Life and work of the Báb**

ON 22 May 1844, an hour before sunset, a memorable encounter took place at Shíráz in southern Persia, between 'Alí-Muḥammad, called the Báb (which means the 'Gate'), a twenty-five-year-old Siyyid (descendant of Muḥammad), and his guest, Mullá Ḥusayn, a scholarly Muslim divine, who had just arrived from Karbilá. Obeying instructions from his teacher, Mullá Ḥusayn had travelled hundreds of miles, fasting and in a devotional attitude, to seek the 'Promised One'. Their conversation lasted till dawn the next morning. Mullá Ḥusayn's account of this unique night reads, in part, as follows:

'I sat spellbound by His utterance, oblivious of time and of those who awaited me. . . . This Revelation, so suddenly and impetuously thrust upon me, came as a thunderbolt which, for a time, seemed to have benumbed my faculties. I was blinded by its dazzling splendour and overwhelmed by its crushing force. Excitement, joy, awe, and wonder stirred the depths of my soul. Predominant among these emotions was a sense of gladness and strength which seemed to have transfigured me. How feeble and impotent, how dejected and timid, I had felt previously! Then I could

---

* For more details of Bahá'í history, see *The Dawn-Breakers* by Nabíl-i-A'ẓam and *God Passes By* by Shoghi Effendi, from which most of the facts in this and the following chapter are taken.

neither write nor walk, so tremulous were my hands and feet. Now, however, the knowledge of His Revelation had galvanized my being. I felt possessed of such courage and power that were the world, all its peoples and its potentates, to rise against me, I would, alone and undaunted, withstand their onslaught. The universe seemed but a handful of dust in my grasp. I seemed to be the Voice of Gabriel personified, calling unto all mankind: "Awake, for, lo! the morning Light has broken. Arise, for His Cause is made manifest. The portal of His grace is open wide; enter therein, O peoples of the world! For He who is your promised One is come!" '[1]

At the time, Mullá Ḥusayn was asked by the Báb not to tell anyone about their meeting or his belief in him. For seventeen other disciples, called the 'Letters of the Living', were to find their way to the Báb spontaneously and without any outside assistance. All eighteen were important personalities, many from the ranks of the clergy. The last but one was a woman, the only one of her sex to be so honoured. She never met the Báb, but a dream, in which he appeared to her, brought her certainty in a Cause for whose truth she and almost all the other Letters of the Living were later to sacrifice their lives. This woman, Zarrín-Táj (Crown of Gold), also known as Ṭáhirih (the Pure One) and Qurratu'l-'Ayn (Solace of the Eyes), is considered the greatest poetess Persia has ever produced.*

---

* Ṭáhirih's importance as a poetess is only surpassed by the contribution she made to the emancipation of women in Persia and throughout the world. Although the embodiment of purity and chastity to all who knew her, at one of the historically most important Bábí conferences she suddenly appeared, adorned and unveiled. This was not only to demonstrate the emancipation of women, but by breaking with Muslim tradition to give visible expression to the significance of the new era and the new teachings. The assembled Bábís were so shocked by her action that

Accompanied by the last disciple, the twenty-two-year-old Quddús, who was highest in rank among the 'Letters', the Báb undertook a long and arduous pilgrimage to Mecca, to proclaim his mission to the Sherif [Sharíf] of the Holy House.* The seventeen other disciples were directed to disperse all over Persia and disseminate their Master's Cause. They showed such heroism in this that the Báb's teaching spread throughout the country like wildfire. Inevitably, the fanatical priesthood, the government and the ignorant masses joined forces against the new teaching; and so began the persecution of the Bábís, as the Báb's followers were called.

Soon after he returned from Mecca, the Báb was arrested near the port of Búshihr and taken to Shíráz, where He was brought before the governor. He was severely rebuked, struck in the face and sentenced to house arrest. He was, however, able to continue his work for a year and a half in relative safety. Meanwhile, because of the agitation growing in the whole country because of his message, even Muham-

---

one of them cut his throat, while others fled and renounced their faith. During the later persecutions of the Bábís, Ṭáhirih died a martyr's death.

When she spoke, the French diplomat and author Comte de Gobineau recorded, 'one felt stirred to the depths of one's soul. . . .' 'The heroism of the lovely but ill-fated poetess of Qasvín . . .', declared Lord Curzon, 'is one of the most affecting episodes in modern history.' 'The appearance of such a woman . . .', wrote the British orientalist E. G. Browne, 'is, in any country and any age, a rare phenomenon, but in such a country as Persia it is a prodigy—nay, almost a miracle. . . . Had the Bábí religion no other claim to greatness, this were sufficient . . . that it produced a heroine like Qurratu'l-'Ayn.'[2]

* The Sherif, one of the highest-ranking clergy in the country, was responsible for the administration of the Ka'bih, a shrine to which all Muslims turn in prayer, and for the care of the hundreds of thousands of pilgrims who visited it every year.

mad S͟háh could no longer afford to ignore the situation. He sent Vaḥíd, one of his most erudite and influential subjects, to S͟híráz. Vaḥíd, who had committed not only the Qur'án to memory but no less than thirty thousand traditions* as well, was to investigate on the spot and report to the S͟háh on the true situation.

Vaḥíd had three interviews with the Báb. In the end he was so overcome by the greatness of the Báb's revelation that he sent a brief report to Ṭihrán, severing his connection with the court and dedicating himself completely to the new Cause. He sacrificed his fortune, his property and, a few years later, his life for that Cause.

Since the tension was increasing everywhere, the governor decided to have the Báb put to death. But this was prevented by the outbreak of a cholera epidemic. The governor fled to the city's outskirts, and was persuaded to release his captive on condition that he leave S͟híráz. The Báb then proceeded to Iṣfáhán. The inhabitants here too were at once captivated by the magic of his personality. Manúc͟hihr K͟hán, the governor of Iṣfáhán, a Christian from Georgia, became one of his followers, and expressed the desire to consecrate all his possessions, valued by contemporaries at forty million francs, to the furtherance of the new Faith; he also declared his intention of converting the S͟háh. The Báb renounced the gift, explaining that by God's Providence the spread of his Cause would be through the blood of the martyrs and not by the aid of earthly goods and power. At the same time he predicted the governor's imminent death, which in fact occurred a few weeks later.

Soon afterwards the Báb was sent from Iṣfáhán to the fortress of Máh-Kú in Ád͟hirbáyján, the remotest northwest corner of the country, where he was imprisoned for

* The sacred traditions of the Muslims.

nine months. When the warden of the fortress acknowledged him and some relaxation in his conditions ensued, he was banished to Chihríq. After being incarcerated there for almost four months, he was taken to Tabríz, where the highest ecclesiastical dignitaries sat in judgment on him, in the presence of the heir to the throne. This gave him the unique opportunity of formally declaring his mission in public, without hindrance. To the question put to him by the president of the court he replied: 'I am, I am, I am the Promised One! I am the One Whose name you have for a thousand years invoked, . . . Whose advent you have longed to witness . . . Verily, I say, it is incumbent upon the peoples of both the East and the West to obey My word, and to pledge allegiance to My person.'[3]

The Báb was sent back to Chihríq, however, kept there for two years, and then taken again to Tabríz, where, on 9 July 1850, he died a martyr's death. On his last day, while talking to his secretary in the cell, an official interrupted the conversation. But the Báb said, 'Not until I have said to him all those things that I wish to say can any earthly power silence Me.'[4] Unimpressed by these words, the official took the secretary away. Then the Báb and one of his most loyal disciples were led to the place of execution. This disciple had previously flung himself at his Master's feet, begging that he should under no circumstances be sent away from him.

The colonel of the Armenian regiment ordered to carry out the execution, a Christian named Sám Khán, turned to the Báb and confessed his uneasy conscience at the painful duty assigned to him. 'Follow your instructions,' the Báb replied, 'and if your intention be sincere, the Almighty is surely able to relieve you of your perplexity.'[5] The Báb and his disciple were suspended from a pillar which divided two rooms of the barracks, facing the square. The firing-squad was ranged in three echelons, each of two-hundred-and-fifty men. Each echelon in turn opened fire until the whole squad had discharged its bullets. The smoke from the seven-hundred-and-fifty rifles was dense and black. When it cleared, the crowd of about ten thousand spectators could hardly believe their eyes. The Báb had disappeared, while his companion stood by the wall, alive and unscathed; only the ropes were in shreds.

The Báb was found, also unhurt, in the same cell he had occupied the night before, and was engaged in completing his interrupted conversation with his secretary. He told the official who entered: 'I have finished My conversation with Siyyid Ḥusayn. Now you may proceed to fulfil your intention.'[6] It was the same official who had come to him before, and now, remembering his earlier cautionary words, the man left the barracks immediately and resigned his post. Sám Khán too dismissed his soldiers at once, swearing that, even if it cost him his life, he would never attempt to repeat the execution. The colonel of the bodyguard volunteered to take over from him. The Báb and his disciple were again tied to the pillar, the new regiment formed in line and opened fire. This time their bodies were riddled with bullets, but their faces remained almost untouched.

The story of the Báb's martyrdom sounds literally incredible, but this account is accepted as historical fact even by enemies of the Bahá'í Faith. A similar account can be found, for instance, in the official Persian history written at the time by order of the Sháh. The events were also confirmed in a letter written on 22 July 1850 (thirteen days after the Báb's death) by Lt.-Col. (later Sir Justin) Sheil, then British Minister in Tihrán, to Lord Palmerston, the Foreign Secretary. (The letter is preserved at the Public Record Office in London.)[7]

The Bahá'ís believe, however, that the miraculous circumstances and signs accompanying the appearance of a Manifestation of God offer no conclusive proof of the truth of his mission. Such proof is offered only by the overwhelming creative Word of God, which is capable of transforming men.

To complete this account of historical events, it should be mentioned that in the year after the Báb's death two-hundred-and-fifty men from the regiment which carried out the execution lost their lives in an earthquake between Ardibíl and Tabríz. Five hundred were shot to death two years later for mutiny. The colonel of the regiment was killed six years after his deed during a bombardment by British naval forces at Muhammarih; while the prime minister, soon after giving the order for the execution on his own responsibility, fell into disfavour, and at the Sháh's command his veins were opened in the bath of the Palace of Fín. Náṣiri'd-Dín Sháh, in whose presence when heir to the throne the Báb was tried and sentenced, was shot dead by one of his enemies in the Mosque at Rayy on the eve of his golden jubilee, which was to have been celebrated throughout Persia with the most elaborate magnificence.

Although the Báb's ministry was confined to six years, we find in history no previous Manifestation of God who produced so many writings as he. Although he had little schooling, and went only for a short time to a teacher, the man refused to continue teaching him because his pupil's questions were beyond him. Later this teacher became a follower of the Báb and suffered martyrdom. One of the Báb's disciples declared before a gathering of clergy that his Master had in his presence revealed within forty-eight hours as many verses as there were in the whole of the Qur'án, which was the result of Muhammad's revelation during a full twenty-two years. The disciple had to pay for these words with his life. In the Persian *Bayán* (Utterance)—his most important work, containing the teachings and laws of the Bábí Revelation—the Báb himself confirms that in the first three years of his ministry he put down in writing no less than five hundred thousand revealed verses. This is more than twenty times as much as the Old and New Testaments contain together. Unfortunately much has been lost through the persecutions of the Bábís; but a good many of his works, as well as letters, missives and prayers, are preserved in the Bahá'í archives at Haifa.*

The new teachings

The central purpose of the Báb was to proclaim the era which would be introduced by the one 'Whom God shall make manifest'—Bahá'u'lláh. That is also why he chose for himself the spiritual name Báb (Gate). All his writings testify to an unqualified devotion to Bahá'u'lláh. In many passages he asks God to accept him as a sacrifice for the great Dispensation to come. According to the Báb's words, the development of history takes place in cycles. With him a new cycle is introduced, reaching its zenith in the revelation of Bahá'u'lláh.†

A striking point in the Báb's writings is that he seldom uses the word 'bad' or 'evil', but speaks of the 'non-good' or 'non-divine'. This indicates that the dualistic principle has been replaced by the principle that there is one spiritual entity, and no absolute evil. The Bahá'ís believe that dark-

---

* The titles of twenty-three of his writings are listed in a recent publication from the Bahá'í World Centre.[8]

† In the words of Shoghi Effendi, the Báb stands 'at the confluence of two universal prophetic cycles, the Adamic Cycle stretching back as far as the first dawnings of the world's recorded religious history and the Bahá'í Cycle destined to propel itself across the unborn reaches of time for a period of no less than five thousand centuries.'[9]

ness is lack of light; cold, lack of warmth. Evil is lack of the good qualities which are revealed to men by the Divine Will as guiding principles for their salvation and spiritual development. The standard of the time is given by the 'living Word of God', that is, through the laws and commandments of the latest divine Manifestation. The words 'devil' and 'Satan' are scarcely to be found in Bahá'í literature, and the only thing called 'devilish' by the Báb, and also by Bahá'u'lláh, is the influence of man's lower nature, which tries to claim all his energies for the satisfaction of its desires and appetites.

As to the idea of God in the Báb's teaching, and also in the Bahá'í Faith, the following words by Bahá'u'lláh give an indication:

'Lauded and glorified art Thou, O Lord, my God! How can I make mention of Thee, assured as I am that no tongue, however deep its wisdom, can befittingly magnify Thy name, nor can the bird of the human heart, however great its longing, ever hope to ascend into the heaven of Thy majesty and knowledge. . . .

'Exalted, immeasurably exalted, art Thou above the strivings of mortal man to unravel Thy mystery, to describe Thy glory, or even to hint at the nature of Thine Essence. For whatever such strivings may accomplish, they never can hope to transcend the limitations imposed upon Thy creatures . . .'[10]

The Báb speaks of three worlds—the world of God, the world of Revelation, and the world of Creation.* The Messengers of God are of two kinds: those who are independent, called Manifestations of God; and the dependent Prophets, who, like the moon, receive their light from the Sun of the Manifestation.

* For further details, see pp. 105–8.

Any attempt to assess the Manifestations of God through human knowledge and by human standards, or to compare one with another, misses the unity and completeness of God's Revelation and leads man astray. Here is the warning of Bahá'u'lláh on this point:

'Beware, O believers in the Unity of God, lest ye be tempted to make any distinction between any of the Manifestations of His Cause, or to discriminate against the signs that have accompanied and proclaimed their Revelation. This indeed is the true meaning of Divine Unity, if ye be of them that apprehend and believe this truth. Be ye assured, moreover, that the works and acts of each and every one of these Manifestations of God, nay whatever pertaineth unto them, and whatsoever they may manifest in the future, are all ordained by God, and are a reflection of His Will and Purpose. Whoso maketh the slightest possible difference between their persons, their words, their messages, their acts and manners, hath indeed disbelieved in God, hath repudiated His signs, and betrayed the Cause of His Messengers.'[11]

The Báb introduced a number of new laws for the individual and for society, and himself anticipated and directed his followers' attention especially to the coming world order of Bahá'u'lláh. Among other things he gave a new calendar based on the solar year, of nineteen months each with nineteen days, which Bahá'u'lláh adopted with certain modifications. The four or five remaining days are placed before the last month, the month of fasting, and are considered as a time of hospitality. The year begins on the day of the vernal equinox (usually 21 March).

Developments in Islám after the Bábí Revelation

Let us now take a brief look at developments in Islám and

its most important schools during the last century. In Írán, the cradle of the Bahá'í Faith, the dynasty of the Qájárs, the mainstay of a degenerate clergy, was overthrown. The clergy, whose influence had often equalled, even surpassed that of the Sháh, lost much respect and power. The overthrow of the Sultanate and Caliphate in Istanbul robbed the Sunnite countries of their symbol of a religious authority; religion was separated from politics and education secularized. Moreover, through contact with the West, Muslim countries have been caught up in a wave of modernism which is materialistic and aims at banishing religion to a place of secondary importance in man's life. For if looked at closely, nationalism, which has overtaken almost all the Muslim countries, is not religious. The best evidence of this is not only the decline in the influence of the clergy and their exclusion from active politics, but also the gradual substitution of the traditional religious system of education by a secular one, and deliberate departure from the letter of the law of Islám.

The unfolding of the Bahá'í Faith

Meanwhile, the Báb's teaching, which reached its fulfilment in the Bahá'í Faith, has overcome the difficulties of its early days. The powers of narrow-mindedness and fanaticism at first succeeded in killing over twenty thousand believers in the cradle of the Faith. To this very day such powers have managed to plague the Bahá'ís and curtail their basic rights. Yet they could not extinguish the flame of the young Faith. Born in Persia, it reached the Holy Land, spread to Egypt and America, and from there to Europe and the whole world. At present, Bahá'u'lláh's teaching has been disseminated in well over three hundred countries, islands and territories. Bahá'í literature is already translated into nearly six hundred languages, and the believers from all nations, races and religions form in their own ranks the units from which a new world order is being built. In April 1975 there were already one-hundred-and-nineteen National Spiritual Assemblies, elected bodies representing the Bahá'ís in various countries (compared to only twelve such bodies in 1953), and by that date there were over 70,000 Bahá'í centres and communities spread throughout the world (compared with 2,500 in 1953).

Today Bahá'u'lláh's teaching is accorded so much significance and weight that many people, even if they do not themselves subscribe to this religion, will nevertheless admit that its Founders are among the noblest figures in religious history and that their teachings are of the greatest importance for the history of mankind. To give only a few examples, Albert Schweitzer, in a letter of 22 March 1953 to the Spiritual Assembly of the Bahá'ís in Stuttgart, expressed his special reverence for Bahá'u'lláh and his teaching, and said that he followed with interest and attention the development of this young religion. Queen Marie of Rumania affirmed her belief in the Bahá'í Faith in these moving words: 'If ever the name of Bahá'u'lláh or 'Abdu'l-Bahá comes to your attention, do not put their writings from you. Search out their Books, and let their glorious, peace-bringing, love-creating words and lessons sink into your hearts as they have into mine. . . . Seek them, and be the happier.'[12]

Arnold Toynbee viewed the young faith as a religion for the future. The eminent Swiss psychiatrist and entomologist, Professor Auguste Forel, wrote in his will: 'In 1920 I learned at Karlsruhe of the supraconfessional world religion of the Bahá'ís, founded in the Orient seventy years ago by a Persian, Bahá'u'lláh. This is the real religion of

"Social Welfare" without dogmas or priests, binding together all men of this small terrestrial globe of ours. I have become a Bahá'í. May this religion live and prosper for the good of humanity! This is my most ardent desire.'[13] In a letter of 1908 Leo Tolstoy wrote: 'The teachings of the Bábís which come to us out of Islám have through Bahá'u'lláh's teachings been gradually developed and now present us with the highest and purest form of religious teaching.' In another passage he said: 'We spend our lives trying to unlock the mystery of the universe; there was a Turkish Prisoner, Bahá'u'lláh, who had the key!'[14]

And how do the Bahá'ís see their own future? Shoghi Effendi, the Guardian of the Bahá'í Faith, concluded his historical work, *God Passes By*, with this paragraph: 'Whatever may befall this infant Faith of God in future decades or in succeeding centuries, whatever the sorrows, dangers and tribulations which the next stage in its world-wide development may engender, from whatever quarter the assaults to be launched by its present or future adversaries may be unleashed against it, however great the reverses and setbacks it may suffer, we, who have been privileged to apprehend, to the degree our finite minds can fathom, the significance of these marvellous phenomena associated with its rise and establishment, can harbour no doubt that what it has already achieved in the first hundred years of its life provides sufficient guarantee that it will continue to forge ahead, capturing loftier heights, tearing down every obstacle, opening up new horizons and winning still mightier victories, until its glorious mission, stretching into the dim ranges of time that lie ahead, is totally fulfilled.'[15]

VII

GOD'S COVENANT FULFILLED

No visible limits

ABOUT a year before the First World War a memorable meeting took place in Paris. The famous philosopher Henri Bergson, who asserted the principle of the *élan vital* in evolution, had asked for and been granted an interview with 'Abdu'l-Bahá at the latter's hotel. Bergson went to the hotel with several of his 'disciples'. They were welcomed by 'Abdu'l-Bahá, who himself poured the tea, then invited Bergson to open the conversation. But the philosopher said this was more proper for his host. So 'Abdu'l-Bahá started by observing that the difference between materialists and those who believed in God was by no means so great as was generally assumed.

The materialists admitted that man had not yet grasped the reality of things, for if he had, there would be no possibility of progress left. For instance, if the essence of iron had been fathomed in its full complexity, this would exclude all further progress in the field of metallurgy. In reality we were meeting new unknowns every day and had to gain new knowledge within our field of cognition. The believers said there was an all-embracing reality which man could not grasp, a force they called divine. If we thought out these two views to their logical conclusion, we would see that they were not far removed from each other.

Bergson replied with a smile that if 'Abdu'l-Bahá wished

to find such common ground between the two parties, he had no objection. ʿAbdu'l-Bahá said that in judging a point, however, one should let justice prevail: Bergson should imagine himself standing on the shores of an immense ocean, not knowing all that was in the ocean or aware of its extent; he might now take a glass of water from it, try it and find that it was salty; could he then assert, regardless of all that was outside his knowledge, that in this vast ocean there was no salt? Bergson thought for a while, then admitted that one could not make that assertion.

ʿAbdu'l-Bahá continued with the observation that we were in a world which was a small part of the infinite universe, with no possibility of exploring everything, nor did we know what levels of life existed. If we considered man as part of the unimaginably great realm of Being, we should find that he was endowed with reason and will. But if we found reason and will in human individuals, would it be right to exclude the possibility that the First Cause from which man had emerged—whether we called it Nature or God—also possessed reason and will?

Valíyu'lláh Varqá,* a Bahá'í present at this interview, who gave me an account of it on two occasions, reported that after these words of ʿAbdu'l-Bahá's there was a complete silence in the room for several minutes. Then Bergson, deeply impressed, said he was surprised there was so simple an explanation for so difficult a question. He rose, bowed, and kissed ʿAbdu'l-Bahá's hand on leaving. His companions followed suit.

Bahá'u'lláh's eldest son

Who was ʿAbdu'l-Bahá? Eldest son of Bahá'u'lláh, he was

---

* Valíyu'lláh Varqá, whose father and brother were among the best-known martyrs of the Bahá'í Faith, was a close confidant of ʿAbdu'l-Bahá and Shoghi Effendi, accompanied the former on several journeys, and was appointed Hand of the Cause of God by the latter.

born in Ṭihrán on 23 May 1844, the same night in which the Báb, Bahá'u'lláh's forerunner, declared his mission to his first disciple. 'Abdu'l-Bahá's life spanned the Heroic Age of the Bahá'í Faith, 1844–1921, and their stories are interwoven at every stage. His grandfather was a minister of state, and he himself lived in very easy circumstances during his early childhood. When he was a few months old, that first disciple brought to his father, Bahá'u'lláh, a letter from the Báb. Bahá'u'lláh, who had already renounced the ministerial position which by the custom of the day he could have inherited from his father, acknowledged the Báb immediately as a Messenger of God, and began to teach his friends and family about the new Cause. It is worth recording that in the visible world there was never, so far as we know, a personal meeting between the Báb and Bahá'u'lláh.

'Abdu'l-Bahá was six years old when the Báb was publicly shot in Tabríz. When he was eight the time of suffering began. Two followers of the Báb, who were obsessed by the execution of their Master and blamed Náṣiri'd-Dín Sháh for his death, made an attempt on the Sháh's life but only injured him slightly. The clergy, the government and the mass of the population now joined forces to destroy the Bábís. Every suspect was arrested and murdered in the most appalling way. An Austrian officer, Captain von Goumoens, wrote to a friend that he never left his house, to avoid meeting with fresh scenes of horror. One Bábí had molten lead poured down his throat, another had his eyes gouged out and an ear cut off, which he was then forced to eat. Another had nine holes incised in his body, burning candles were thrust into these and he was marched through the streets to his death, after which his body was cut in two and its two halves were impaled on the city gate.[1]

Bahá'u'lláh himself was imprisoned. A chain weighing

over fifty kilogrammes* was put round his neck, the marks of which he bore till the end of his life. There were a number of other Bábís in prison with him. Every now and then a few of them were taken out and murdered in some atrocious manner. At the age of eight, 'Abdu'l-Bahá had to leave his father's house and the rich care-free life of his childhood. The house was looted and burned down. The family was bereft of almost all its friends. Finally Bahá'u'lláh and several Bábís were released, since it transpired that they had nothing to do with the assassination attempt, but only on condition that they leave Persia and go into exile. So in midwinter and without adequate clothing they set out on the long and difficult journey to Baghdád, which took several months. As a result, with almost all their leading men killed or expelled, the Bábís became completely dejected. Their vitality, and the strength of character they had previously shown, were weakened, and some of them even began to sow discord among the believers.

Bahá'u'lláh proclaims his mission

Distressed and saddened by the conditions surrounding him, a year after his arrival in Baghdád Bahá'u'lláh withdrew into the solitude of the mountains, and nobody knew at the time where he was living. When eventually, after two years, his family and friends heard news of him and implored him to return, he acceded to their request, extending once again his guidance and encouragement to the Bábís. In the course of time he succeeded in forming a community which was greatly respected by the population.

But the Persian consul-general in Baghdád, alarmed by Bahá'u'lláh's growing influence and incited by Shaykh 'Abdu'l-Ḥusayn, a jealous priest, worked for some months

* Well over a hundred pounds.

to persuade his government to take measures against him and his companions. Rumours abounded, and those in his immediate entourage felt anxious and uncertain. Yet Bahá'u'lláh chose precisely this period to declare himself as the one promised by the Báb and all earlier Messengers of God. Thus the days of uncertainty were transformed into days of joy and beauty, and became one of the most important periods in the experience of the Bahá'ís, as the followers of Bahá'u'lláh in time came to be known.

Bahá'u'lláh himself says: 'Rejoice with exceeding gladness, O people of Bahá, as ye call to remembrance the Day of supreme felicity, the Day whereon the Tongue of the Ancient of Days hath spoken, as He departed from His House, proceeding to the Spot from which He shed upon the whole of creation the splendours of His name, the All-Merciful. . . . Were We to reveal the hidden secrets of that Day, all they that dwell on earth and in the heavens would swoon away and die, except such as will be preserved by God, the Almighty, the All-Knowing, the All-Wise.

'Such is the inebriating effect of the words of God upon Him Who is the Revealer of His undoubted proofs, that His pen can move no longer.'[2]

Bahá'u'lláh's exile

Bahá'u'lláh, with his family and companions, was banished from Baghdád to Constantinople. After a few months he was sent from there to Adrianople, whose population included very many Christians, and it was hoped that the flame of the new Faith would in this way die down of its own accord. 'Abdu'l-Bahá was then nineteen. In Adrianople the traditional enemies of the Bahá'ís—the Muslim clergy, their superstitious and fanatical supporters among the people, as well as the governments of Persia and the Ottoman

Empire—banded together against Bahá'u'lláh. They were incited by a few renegade Bábís who joined them for base motives, began to slander him before the government, and tried to murder him in the public bath. When this attempt failed, one of them mixed poison into his food, after which Bahá'u'lláh lay severely ill for over a month. As the slanders persisted, the Ottoman government decided to destroy completely the cause of the Bahá'ís. It was during these days that Bahá'u'lláh wrote a number of his famous Tablets, in which he addressed kings and rulers, severally and collectively, ecclesiastical leaders, high officials of government and others, admonishing them to fear God and to heed his message:

'Ye are but vassals, O kings of the earth! He Who is the King of Kings hath appeared, arrayed in His most wondrous glory, and is summoning you unto Himself, the Help in Peril, the Self-Subsisting. Take heed lest pride deter you from recognizing the Source of Revelation . . . We see you rejoicing in that which ye have amassed for others and shutting out yourselves from the worlds which naught except My guarded Tablet can reckon. . . . Wash from your hearts all earthly defilements, and hasten to enter the Kingdom of your Lord, the Creator of earth and heaven . . .'[3]

The Ottoman government's plan was to separate Bahá'u'lláh from his supporters and it was rumoured that they would be banished to different places. One of the believers who heard of this attempted to do away with himself. In the end the government was persuaded to deport them all together, and the penal colony of 'Akká was chosen as their place of banishment.* At that time 'Akká was the worst

---

* A few of the renegade Bábís were sent with Bahá'u'lláh to 'Akká, while four of his loyal companions were exiled to Cyprus with others who had opposed him.

prison in the Ottoman Empire, a terminal station for criminals who could never be allowed to return to human society.

The conditions in this prison were indescribable. Think of some eighty people crammed into a very small space, without water for drinking or washing, without enough food, without beds or other furniture, tormented by malaria, typhoid and dysentery, in a heat impossible for many Europeans to imagine. Among them were babies and their mothers, the aged and the sick. Bahá'u'lláh called the place the 'Most Great Prison', and said that such immense sufferings and affliction had not been heard of since 'the foundation of the world'.[4]

Most of the exiles fell sick. 'Abdu'l-Bahá nursed them until he himself collapsed under this burden from sheer exhaustion. It is a miracle that only a few of the prisoners died and most regained their health, although this terrible state of affairs lasted two years with almost no contact with the outer world. But gradually as it was realized, both by the governors of 'Akká and some of its citizens, that the prisoners were good and loving people, more freedom was granted and pilgrims were allowed to come. Now Bahá'u'lláh sent his Tablets in all directions; his 'Most Holy Book', containing his laws and ordinances,* was also revealed in 'Akká. Meanwhile his followers were carrying his teachings into thirteen countries.

'Abdu'l-Bahá: The Centre of the Covenant

'The Sun of Bahá has set'—so ran a telegram sent to the Ottoman Sulṭán on 29 May 1892; after forty years of imprisonment and exile Bahá'u'lláh had passed from this world. At this time 'Abdu'l-Bahá was forty-eight. By Bahá'u'lláh's testament, which he called *The Book of My*

* *Kitáb-i-Aqdas.*

Covenant, 'Abdu'l-Bahá had been appointed 'Centre of the Covenant' and the authorized interpreter of his father's teachings. It was to him the Bahá'ís should turn in all their affairs. Although still under the government's strict supervision, he preserved the contacts made all over the world and exchanged letters with the believers in all continents. Sometimes, too, he received bad news of the severe persecutions to which the Bahá'ís in Persia were still being subjected; sometimes as many as three hundred were martyred on a single day.

In 1907 the Ottoman government sent a commission of four officers to 'Akká, to determine whether charges brought before the government by 'Abdu'l-Bahá's enemies were justified. As they had come to investigate his case, 'Abdu'l-Bahá sought no contact with them, so that they should not gain the impression he wished to influence them in any way. This was held against him, however, as lack of courtesy, and their eventual report, based on many statements and testimonies by his enemies, said that he was to be regarded as an enemy of the people, the government, and religion. The leader of the commission announced that he would soon be returning to 'Akká, and would then have 'Abdu'l-Bahá crucified at the city gate. At this time there was also an abortive attempt on 'Abdu'l-Bahá's life: three bullets were fired at him in the darkness, but all missed.

Soon afterwards the Young Turks' Revolution broke out. The Sulṭán was taken prisoner, two members of the commission were killed, one was exiled, and the fourth fled with his servant to Alexandria. When the servant saw that his master's star had set, he took his luggage and all his money and disappeared. The Páshá, who dared not disclose his identity to anybody and was completely without means, came to a Bahá'í and said he was one of those who had been most hostile to the Bahá'ís' master; he begged for forgiveness and help. The Bahá'í gave him thirty piastres and reported the incident to 'Abdu'l-Bahá, who at once sent off a larger sum, telling his friends with a smile that this Páshá had formerly worked very long and hard compiling a file, sometimes not sleeping at night—and now this 'unreasonable' Bahá'í wanted to compensate him for everything with thirty piastres![5]

When 'Abdu'l-Bahá, now sixty-four, had regained his freedom, after a sojourn in Egypt he undertook a brief visit to London and Paris, followed in 1912–13 by an extensive journey through North America and Europe. He gave addresses, meeting the press and Bahá'ís, in over forty American cities, fifty-five times in New York alone. In meetings with materialists he talked of the reality of the spirit and expounded proofs of the existence of God; in the synagogues he testified to the genuineness of the mission of Jesus Christ; and in Christian churches he spoke of Muḥammad. He gave addresses to pacifists, Theosophists and Esperantists, in universities, colleges and women's societies. For many who saw him, those meetings were the greatest event in their lives. In his addresses he gave last-minute warning* to the proud Westerners that they would gain nothing by increasing their armaments; they should direct their energies instead to realizing the unity of mankind.

In 1921, when 'Abdu'l-Bahá left this world at the age of seventy-eight, he was accompanied to his last resting-place by over ten thousand people. According to eyewitness reports Palestine had never before seen such a funeral. Jews, Christians and Muslims comforted one another. But the

---

* Before the outbreak of the First World War.

Bahá'ís had lost more than all the others. For to them 'Abdu'l-Bahá was not only the authorized interpreter of Bahá'u'lláh's teachings, not only the Centre of his Covenant, but above all the exemplar of a perfect life. When a Bahá'í today is in a difficult situation and does not know what to do, he asks himself what 'Abdu'l-Bahá would have done in such a case. 'Abdu'l-Bahá occupies in the Bahá'í Faith a unique and exalted position. He received no tuition from any other teacher than Bahá'u'lláh and owed his training and education solely to him. About 'Abdu'l-Bahá, the Guardian of the Bahá'í Faith, Shoghi Effendi, has written these remarkable words:

'He is, and should for all time be regarded, first and foremost, as the Centre and Pivot of Bahá'u'lláh's peerless and all-enfolding Covenant . . . the perfect Exemplar of His teachings . . . the Mainspring of the Oneness of Humanity, the Ensign of the Most Great Peace . . . He is, above and beyond these appellations, the "Mystery of God"—an expression by which Bahá'u'lláh Himself has chosen to designate Him, and which, while it does not by any means justify us to assign to him the station of Prophethood, indicates how in the person of 'Abdu'l-Bahá the incompatible characteristics of a human nature and superhuman knowledge and perfection have been blended and are completely harmonized.'[6]

'Abdu'l-Bahá's maxim can be summed up in the words: everything universal is divine, everything limited is earthly.

If anyone really practised the commandments of the Sermon on the Mount, it was 'Abdu'l-Bahá. This is acknowledged even by many enemies of the Bahá'í Faith. The prime minister, for instance, of the empire in which 'Abdu'l-Bahá had been an exile and a prisoner for fifty-four years, sent an official message 'to extend his sympathy to the family of His Holiness ʿAbduʾl-Bahá in their bereavement.'[7]

The writings ʿAbduʾl-Bahá left are vast in number. They start with a commentary on an important Islamic traditional text, which he wrote at the age of thirteen. Then there are thousands of missives, letters, addresses, expositions and prayers, not all of which have yet been collected. He had the gift of presenting and explaining the most difficult questions in a very simple manner. Laura Clifford Barney (the late Madame Dreyfus-Barney), an American who had the privilege of visiting ʿAbduʾl-Bahá at ʿAkká, asked him many questions at table. His answers, relating to all realms of spiritual and practical life, are collected in her book *Some Answered Questions*. This book not only gives the reader an impression of how ʿAbduʾl-Bahá brought home to his audiences the most profound truths; it also shows the attitude of the Baháʾí Faith to the most varied theological and philosophical problems.

The materialists say man is a product of his environment. They add that he has developed from the animal, as the animal kingdom has evolved from the kingdom of the plants, and that the origin of everything is pure matter. To this the Baháʾís reply that we men have taken a glass of water from the vast ocean whose dimensions we cannot fathom—and have found salt in it.* We cling to this salt, to the life of a man who never went to school, who accompanied his father into exile and prison at the age of nine, and was sixty-four years old when he regained his freedom. Although with his family and his friends he had endured all the vileness and cruelty that a human brain can possibly contrive, his thoughts revolved only around love, forgiveness and the

---

* See p. 83.

unity of mankind. 'There are imperfections in every human being', he said, 'and you will always become unhappy if you look toward the people themselves. But if you look toward God you will love them and be kind to them, for the world of God is the world of perfection and complete mercy. Therefore do not look at the shortcomings of anybody; see with the sight of forgiveness.'[8]

VIII

CHRIST

Jesus and Christendom

WHEN Jesus Christ left this world, there are said to have been about one-hundred-and-twenty people who acknowledged him. But already at that time the believers, even the apostles, differed about the station which Christ occupied. In the first centuries, however, the question remained in the background. The Christians were exposed during this period to continual persecutions by the Jews and the Romans. They were therefore obliged to meet and preach their Lord's doctrine secretly. This pressure from outside created in the believers a strong inner bond and unity, although there were among them different interpretations of Christ's position.

But when Constantine had recognized Christianity as a religion with equal or even preferential rights, the necessity of establishing a dogma about the statements on Christ's significance made itself more and more felt. Theological differences had arisen, and two parties faced each other in sharp opposition. Constantine, regarding this theological conflict as unimportant, at first hesitated to act. It became clear, however, that such inaction would have disastrous consequences, since the parties threatened to destroy the unity of Christendom. So the Emperor felt obliged to summon all the bishops, in order to reach a decision and protect the unity of the Church and the Roman Empire. In

A.D. 325 a Council met in Nicaea, which in the history of Christendom is recorded as the first oecumenical council. At this gathering, after heated discussions, the majority of the bishops accepted the doctrine of the essential unity of God and Christ. Anyone of a different opinion was at first cautioned, afterwards declared a heretic, and banished.

In spite of this the theological conflict went on: literally about a 'jot or tittle'. For jot is the Greek letter *iota*, and one party adhered to the formulation *homoousios* (the same in substance), while the other wanted to have the relation between Father and Son described as *homoiousios* (similar in substance). In the following centuries there were many further disputes within the Christian religion, concerning the relationship between the two natures in Christ, the divine and the human, which led to profound divisions. This quarrel had originally broken out over the question of whether Mary could be called only Mother of Christ, or Mother of God as well. In later centuries the argument as to whether the Holy Ghost emanated from the Father alone or from Father and Son became one of the reasons for the separation of the Roman from the Eastern Church. Similar theological differences, especially over the mother of Jesus Christ, are still being argued today by the main Churches; and the conceptions of Christ's position are still divergent. All things considered, if we leave details out of account, we may say that the overwhelming majority of Christians today believe in the consubstantiality (essential unity) of God and Christ.

The Qur'án and the Christology of the Church

This basic dogma of Christian theology was firmly rejected by Muḥammad, as the following texts from the Qur'án illustrate:

> In the Name of God, the Compassionate, the Merciful
> Say: He is God alone:
> God the eternal!
> He begetteth not, and He is not begotten;
> And there is none like unto Him.[1]

And again:

> Yet they say, 'The God of Mercy hath begotten issue from the angels.'
> Glory be to Him! Nay, they are but His honoured servants: They speak not till He hath spoken; and they do His bidding.
> He knoweth what is before them and what is behind them; and no plea shall they offer
> Save for whom He pleaseth; and they tremble for fear of Him.[2]

Muḥammad used even sharper words in Súrih IX:

> The Jews say, 'Ezra is a son of God'; and the Christians say, 'The Messiah is a son of God.' Such the sayings in their mouths! They resemble the saying of the Infidels of old! God do battle with them! How are they misguided!
> They take their teachers, and their monks, and the Messiah, son of Mary, for Lords beside God, though bidden to worship one God only.[3]

Súrih XIX contains words of similar harshness:

> They say: 'The God of Mercy hath gotten offspring.' Now have ye done a monstrous thing!
> Almost might the very Heavens be rent thereat, and the Earth cleave asunder, and the mountains fall down in fragments,
> That they ascribe a son to the God of Mercy, when it beseemeth not the God of Mercy to beget a son!
> Verily there is none in the Heavens and in the Earth but shall approach the God of Mercy as a servant. He hath taken note of them, and numbered them with exact numbering:

And each of them shall come to Him, on the day of Resurrection, singly: . . .[4]

Many more of these texts could be produced, both from the Qur'án and the traditions of Islám, rejecting in unmistakable language any incarnation of God. This is also why Christian and Islamic theologians have been at cross purposes when discussing the most essential issues of religion.

Man and the Manifestations of God

What are the particular aspects to be taken into account when investigating the progressive development of God's revelation? What facts is it absolutely essential to consider when we attempt to come to terms with such complex questions as the station and nature of Christ? The essence of the revelation of God and the station of Christ are problems which from the outset entail a danger of speculation. Anyone concerned with them should be aware of the limits imposed on our powers. In this connection I would make the following points:

(1) Man has not been given any capacity to describe transcendental truths directly. When we wish to make statements about spiritual things, we can only use our concrete ideas from the realm of the senses. If we say, 'This is a great man', we mean in a spiritual way, but our description must be drawn from the world of the senses. It is the same when we talk of 'progress' or say that some one is spiritually 'on a high level'. In human language there is indeed not a single word which could explain a direct spiritual concept. Instead, every spiritual statement must use the mantle of what can be registered by the senses. This is why Christ spoke in parables, because we cannot understand any other language.

Consider, for instance, the expression 'Mouthpiece of

God'. Now imagine a man holding a tube to his mouth and speaking through it: God is in the man's place, and the tube, the mouthpiece of God, is the Revealer. It is just the same with the concept 'Son of God': this too is meant to express a spiritual relationship in a language within the grasp of our senses, and so the phrase 'Son of God' is used as a symbol of something which we can never fully comprehend. But it is by no means the case that the term 'Son of God' has been applied only to Christ. Apart from the Old Testament, where men are several times referred to as 'sons of God',* in St. John's Gospel we read: 'But as many as received him, to them gave he power to become the sons of God, even to them that believe on his name: Which were born, not of blood, nor of the will of the flesh, nor of the will of man, but of God.'[5] True believers and apostles are thus acknowledged in the Bible as 'children of God', who are seen metaphorically as begotten by God Himself.

(2) When we consider the position and nature of a Manifestation of God, in this case Jesus Christ, we must always bear in mind that in principle a lower stage in creation cannot grasp the nature of a higher. Vegetables have no 'understanding' of the qualities which characterize animals; animals cannot understand man as a reasoning being; and we men must not imagine we can describe in human terms and expressions the true relation between Christ, the Revealers, and God.

(3) Man has no direct relation to the Word of God. His understanding of the Holy Scriptures differs, therefore, according to humanity's stage of development. Different denominations produce different and often opposite inter-

---

* '. . . the sons of God saw the daughters of men . . .' (Genesis vi, 2); '. . . the Lord hath said unto me, Thou art my Son; this day have I begotten thee . . .' (Psalms ii, 7).

pretations of the same holy text. So we must learn to distinguish between the Holy Scriptures themselves and our understanding of them. We should also remember that the Word of God is put before us in the garb of human language, which is subject to continual change. The Manifestations of God cannot speak to us in God's language, but are obliged to use ours. Accordingly, the Manifestation's knowledge is not confined to what is given in his revelation: Moses knew more than is recorded in the Old Testament, Jesus than is recorded in the New. Each Messenger of God, drawing from the infinite Kingdom of Revelation, must take account of the limitations of men in his particular age and adapt himself to them.

Sometimes, indeed, enlightening words are needed from the succeeding Revealer, to unravel the meaning of certain sayings and parables in the previous Dispensation and to 'unseal' the 'wine' of those truths which are obscure. But to identify the Revealers with what is communicated to us orally, in writing or through the story of their lives, is to ignore their high rank, deny their unity and detract from their spiritual sovereignty.

(4) In modern times man no longer tries to make any statements about the essence of things. We have become more modest. We have recognized that the statements we make can at best concern only the qualities, signs and appearances of things. The philosopher refrains from discussing the objective world. The physicist too has become used to the fact that he cannot reach any absolutely exact result when measuring a physical process, because the very act of measurement influences that result. We are fully aware, therefore, that we cannot make any statement about the essence of a piece of wood or iron. If this is the situation in the physical realm, how can man hope to make

permanently binding statements on the substance of Divinity and of Christ, or to judge whether the two are the same or similar in substance!

'So perfect and comprehensive is His [God's] creation', writes Bahá'u'lláh, 'that no mind nor heart, however keen or pure, can ever grasp the nature of the most insignificant of His creatures; much less fathom the mystery of Him Who is the Day-Star of Truth, Who is the invisible and unknowable Essence. The conceptions of the devoutest of mystics, the attainments of the most accomplished amongst men, the highest praise which human tongue or pen can render, are all the product of man's finite mind and are conditioned by its limitations.'[6]

(5) If we compare Jesus's statements about himself as handed down in the New Testament, we see that they are not all of the same kind. We find passages where he says, 'he that hath seen me hath seen the Father . . . Believest thou not that I am in the Father, and the Father in me?'[7] But we also find verses saying, '. . . the word which ye hear is not mine, but the Father's which sent me'[8] or 'my Father is greater than I.'[9] Elsewhere he shows even greater humility in describing his relationship to the Father when he admonishes a would-be disciple who has called him 'Good Master': 'Why callest thou me good? There is none good but one, that is, God.'[10] About his return, too, he says, 'But of that day and that hour knoweth no man, no, not the angels which are in heaven, neither the Son, but the Father.'[11]

Christ illustrated his relationship to the Father through a great many different images, in which his own position ranges from one of extreme modesty to that of complete divinity. Perhaps with each parable he was trying to reveal to us a new aspect of that relationship. How can it be right, then, for man to turn this many-coloured picture into a dull monotone through a rigid dogma? And what could justify him in assuming that the truth is exhausted by such a dogma and that the faith or unbelief of all mankind is dependent on the affirmation or denial of this wording which is declared to be binding?

(6) If man has lost his living, spiritual relation to the object of his faith, there is no longer any difference between faith and superstition. If a faith is based on speculations, no criticism can be made of an African who carves himself a wooden idol and worships this as creator. The mass of religious speculations produces an inflexible net, which leaves the living faith no more scope for development. Such faith shines out in action and attitude, in continual fear of God, through testing and purification; attempts to express it in words come second.

The Revealers' testimony about themselves

Bahá'u'lláh teaches that all the Messengers of God spoke of themselves in three ways: as God, as Mediator, and as man. All the sacred writings of the great religions can be examined from this viewpoint, and the same three aspects will always be found. In the Old Testament there are passages where Moses speaks of himself as 'I, thy Lord', others where he describes himself as 'God's messenger', and finally those in which he identifies himself with humble man. I have already shown how these three aspects apply to Christ. Even Muḥammad, who rejects so sharply the belief that Christ as the Son of God is the incarnation of God, is recorded in a well-known traditional text as saying: 'I and God have various relations, sometimes I am He and He is I.'[12] The Qur'án in particular shows how in various passages Muḥammad addresses himself to men with absolute divine authority, while in others he speaks as a 'Messenger of God' or as a man.

This is why in the Qur'án, as in the Old Testament, we very often find the words, 'And We said', or 'And God said . . .'

So even in Islám the possibility was open for the development of theological schools which identified the Revealer with God. Indeed, despite Muḥammad's urgent warnings, quite an important Muslim school has developed which believes in consubstantiality between ʿAlí, the first Imám, and God—a development which later encouraged some of the Ṣúfís to make the extreme assertion that in states of ecstasy they could claim absolute divinity for themselves. The Bahá'í scholar Mírzá Abu'l-Faḍl has described this assertion as a cancerous growth in the body of religion.

Why have the Messengers of God spoken of themselves in these three fashions? ʿAbdu'l-Bahá gives us an illuminating explanation: If we compare Divinity with the sun, the Messenger of God is like a pure and perfect mirror in which the sun is reflected. Now, the mirror in referring to the sun might say of itself: 'The sun is in me', or 'I am a reflector of the sun', or 'I am a fragile mirror'. Bahá'u'lláh teaches that all God's Messengers appear from the same source and work within a divine plan for the education, ennoblement and redemption of humanity. It is not for us as men to assess and grade their value, to declare Christ more important than Moses or Moses than Abraham. Rather must we see them all in the light of unity.

As the words spoken by each Messenger, and also the signs and events accompanying his mission, were conditioned by time and adapted to circumstances, we have no criteria by which to apprehend these Messengers' true greatness, let alone compare them with each other. Each Messenger has therefore looked upon himself as the embodiment of Revelation, as Revelation itself. Bahá'u'lláh says: 'Contemplate with thine inward eye the chain of successive

Revelations that hath linked the Manifestation of Adam with that of the Báb. I testify before God that each one of these Manifestations hath been sent down through the operation of the Divine Will and Purpose, that each hath been the bearer of a specific Message, that each hath been entrusted with a divinely-revealed Book and been commissioned to unravel the mysteries of a mighty Tablet. The measure of the Revelation with which every one of them hath been identified had been definitely fore-ordained.'[13]

'I am Adam,' says Muḥammad in one traditional text, 'I am Noah, I am Abraham, I am Moses, I am Christ.'* And in another passage: 'I am the embodiment of the prophets.'[14] Christ says, 'Before Abraham was, I am' or 'I am the way, the truth, and the life: no man cometh unto the Father, but by me.'[15]

But instead of taking these words as a sign of the unity of the Messengers of God, the clergy of the different great religions have interpreted them as evidence of each Revealer's claim to uniqueness. Yet the New Testament offers some conclusive indications of the unity of the Revealers. In John's Gospel, for instance, it says: 'And this is the record of John [the Baptist], when the Jews sent priests and Levites from Jerusalem to ask him, Who art thou? And he confessed, and denied not; but confessed, I am not the Christ. And they asked him, What then? Art thou Elias [Elijah]? And he saith, I am not. Art thou that prophet? And he answered, No.'[16] In Matthew's Gospel, however, we read: 'And his disciples asked him [Christ], saying, Why then say the scribes that Elias must first come? And Jesus answered and said unto them, Elias truly shall first come, and

---

* Súrih ii, 285 in the Qur'án is also to be understood in the sense of the unity of the Manifestations of God: 'We make no distinction between the Messengers.'

restore all things. But I say unto you, That Elias is come already, and they knew him not, but have done unto him whatsoever they listed. Likewise shall also the Son of man suffer of them. Then the disciples understood that he spake unto them of John the Baptist.'[17]

So John the Baptist denied that he was Elijah, whereas Christ hinted that he had been. It might be suggested, of course, that Christ did not *know*, that John made a mistake, or that the disciples misunderstood the allusion. The right interpretation, however, is that each Messenger of God is also his predecessor returned, even if a completely new outpouring of the divine truth is connected with his mission. In this context Bahá'u'lláh offers the image that if today's 'Sun of Revelation' should assert that he was yesterday's sun, then he is right. But if, considering the difference between the qualities and strength of the rays and warmth radiated, he should assert that he was not yesterday's sun, this is equally true. That is how the unity and distinctiveness of the Messengers of God should be understood.

Jesus never claimed finality for his mission, for he stated expressly, 'I have yet many things to say unto you, but ye cannot bear them now. Howbeit when he, the Spirit of truth, is come, he will guide you into all truth: for he shall not speak of himself; but whatsoever he shall hear, that shall he speak: and he will shew you things to come.'[18]

By this he meant that his teaching was neither final nor absolute but adapted to the capacities of his hearers, and that more would be said later. There is nothing in history to suggest that the 'Spirit of truth' spoke once for all time to the disciples at Whitsun, or that the Christian churches have since then been guided into all truth. George Townshend, sometime Canon of St. Patrick's Cathedral in Dublin and Archdeacon of Clonfert, writes: 'Christ himself never made the assertion that He was "the Promised One of All Ages" or "the Lord of Hosts"; nor did any of the apostles, nor indeed is it to be found in the Bible. Peter's mighty declaration of faith on which the Christian Church is built [Matt. xvi, 16] is simply that "Thou art the Christ, the Son of the Living God".'[19]

The return promised by Christ is understood by the Bahá'ís as the promise of a new revelation, and they take the various images which Jesus used in proclaiming his future return in the sense of the mirror analogy mentioned above.* Thus he says at one time, 'I come again', but at a different time, 'There cometh another', and elsewhere he speaks of the coming of the Redeemer, the Holy Ghost, or the Lord of the Vineyard.

The station of the Revealers of God

To the Bahá'ís, the Messengers of God are not simply men who have been given a specific mission from God; rather, on the ladder of creation, they belong to a kingdom which is 'not of this world'. They are a species *sui generis*.

For a better appreciation of the Bahá'í view, I should explain that three worlds of being are to be distinguished:†

---

* See p. 102.

† Despite this necessary distinction, the fundamental connection and unity of the realm of reality must not be ignored. Bahá'u'lláh says: 'How wondrous is the unity of the Living, the Ever-Abiding God—a unity which is exalted above all limitations, that transcendeth the comprehension of all created things! He hath, from everlasting, dwelt in His inaccessible habitation of holiness and glory, and will unto everlasting continue to be enthroned upon the heights of His independent sovereignty and grandeur. . . . From the exalted source, and out of the essence of His favour and bounty He hath entrusted every created thing with a sign of His knowledge, so that none of His creatures may be deprived of its share in expressing, each according to its capacity and rank, this knowledge. . . . Every created thing will be enabled . . . to reveal

(1) That of the reality of God which is beyond our conceiving. Of this Bahá'u'lláh writes: 'He is, and hath from everlasting been, one and alone, without peer or equal, eternal in the past, eternal in the future, detached from all things, ever-abiding, unchangeable and self-subsisting. . . . Any and every comparison is applicable only to His creatures, and all conceptions of association are conceptions that belong solely to those that serve Him. Immeasurably exalted is His Essence above the descriptions of His creatures. He, alone, occupieth the Seat of transcendent majesty, of supreme and inaccessible glory.'[21] Imám 'Alí comments on the relationship between man and this world of God's absolute reality: 'The way is barred and to seek it is impiety . . .'[22] This is also what Jesus Christ meant by the words: 'No man cometh unto the Father', and then, referring to the second world, 'but by me'.[23]

(2) The Kingdom of Divine Revelation, the Kingdom of God or of Heaven.* It is from this spiritual realm that the Manifestations of God appear—who make known 'the Divine' to man (but are not an incarnation of God), to enable him to have a share in eternal life. Bahá'u'lláh says: 'The door of the knowledge of the Ancient of Days being thus closed in the face of all beings, the Source of

---

the potentialities of its pre-ordained station, will recognize its capacity and limitations, and will testify to the truth that "He, verily, is God; there is none other God besides Him".'[20]

* In the great religions of revelation, terms like Heaven, the Kingdom of Heaven, etc., sometimes refer to the Kingdom of Revelation which represents this second world of being. There are also passages where the terms are used for the realm to which the believing soul finds access after its separation from the body. Heaven on earth, or the Kingdom of God on earth, is the description of our world in a future state of maturity. It is to be identified with the basic spiritual unity of mankind and with true peace.

infinite grace . . . hath caused those luminous Gems of Holiness to appear out of the realm of the spirit, in the noble form of the human temple, and be made manifest unto all men, that they may impart unto the world the mysteries of the unchangeable Being, and tell of the subtleties of His imperishable Essence.

'These sanctified Mirrors, these Day-Springs of ancient glory, are, one and all, the Exponents on earth of Him Who is the central Orb of the universe, its Essence and ultimate Purpose. From Him proceed their knowledge and power; from Him is derived their sovereignty. The beauty of their countenance is but a reflection of His image, and their revelation a sign of His deathless glory. They are the Treasuries of Divine knowledge, and the Repositories of celestial wisdom. Through them is transmitted a grace that is infinite, and by them is revealed the Light that can never fade . . .'[24] He also says: 'He Who is everlastingly hidden from the eyes of men can never be known except through His Manifestation, and His Manifestation can adduce no greater proof of the truth of His Mission than the proof of His own Person.'[25]

'Abdu'l-Bahá says: '. . . the Kingdom is not a material place, it is sanctified from time and place. It is a spiritual world, a divine world, and the centre of the Sovereignty of God; it is freed from body and that which is corporeal, and it is purified and sanctified from the imaginations of the human world.'[26]

The unity of the Manifestations of God, which amounts also to the fundamental unity of religions, is thus *a priori*, since all the Manifestations of God belong to the Kingdom of Revelation. That is why in all the great religions, side by side with the teachings and commandments which differ according to factors conditioned by place and time, we find common universal truths which link them throughout the ages. Because of this common origin of divine revelation man is not permitted to reject a Manifestation of God, who is the embodiment of divine authority, and whose knowledge is neither conditioned nor acquired.*

(3) The world of creation, including minerals, the vegetable kingdom, the animal kingdom and mankind. On this plane man is the crown of creation. 'Abdu'l-Bahá says: 'Man is the highest work of creation, the nearest to God of all creatures.'[27]

Bahá'u'lláh says: 'Man is the supreme Talisman. Lack of a proper education hath, however, deprived him of that which he doth inherently possess. Through a word proceeding out of the mouth of God he was called into being; by one word more he was guided to recognize the Source of his education; by yet another word his station and destiny were safeguarded.'[28]

In another passage he writes: 'How lofty is the station which man, if he but choose to fulfil his high destiny, can attain! To what depths of degradation he can sink, depths which the meanest of creatures have never reached!'[29] On the qualities and powers latent in the human soul Bahá'u'lláh says: '. . . the human soul is, in its essence, one of the signs of God, a mystery among His mysteries. It is one of the mighty signs of the Almighty, the harbinger that proclaimeth the reality of all the worlds of God. Within it lieth concealed that which the world is now utterly incapable of apprehending.'[30]

---

* The Bahá'ís distinguish the independent Manifestations of God from the dependent prophets (such as the Hebrew prophets), who, like the moon from the sun, receive their light and strength from the sun of the Manifestation, and pass them on to man.

The Revelation of God and theologians

The Bahá'ís are convinced that the pure source of revelation has been obscured in all religions during the various historical developments they have undergone, by human embroideries, misunderstandings and misinterpretations on the part of their theologians. This is also the reason why no Messenger of God who has appeared on this earth has yet been accepted by the priesthood of the preceding religion. Whenever these holy beings appeared, they were opposed, persecuted, exiled, imprisoned, killed or crucified, because the divines believed themselves in possession of a criterion by which they could recognize the Promised One. They presumed that their theology must lead to the new living Word of God. But in fact the Messengers of God have always come to free religion from human falsifications and to proclaim something 'for the future'.

Let us consider two New Testament texts from this viewpoint. In the Gospel of Luke, Christ asks one of his disciples: '. . . when the Son of man cometh, shall he find faith on the earth?'[31] This suggests that he will definitely return and will quite certainly not be acknowledged. In I Corinthians Paul says: 'Therefore judge nothing before the time, until the Lord come, who . . . will bring to light the hidden things of darkness . . .'[32] By this he meant that the truth can only be disclosed by the Revelation of God. Only the clarifying words of the New Testament create a true relationship to the Scripture of the Old Testament. It is only Bahá'u'lláh who unseals the divine wine of hidden meanings, and everything must be considered in the light of this new enunciation of eternal truth. The formulation of any dogma is basically a 'judgment' against which Paul gave his warning. It is not the study of theology but the inner readiness to disengage if necessary from the traditional doctrines, dogmas and sayings accepted as correct until then—it is that readiness which, as Bahá'u'lláh stresses, creates receptivity to the new rays of the 'Sun of Truth' and the new Word of God.

Christ: The 'Essence of Being'

Bahá'u'lláh speaks of Jesus Christ as the 'Essence of Being' and 'Lord of the visible and invisible'.[33] Shoghi Effendi described as follows the basic attitude of the Bahá'í to Christ: '. . . the Sonship and Divinity of Jesus Christ are fearlessly asserted, . . . the divine inspiration of the Gospel is fully recognized . . .'[34] (See pp. 101–2.)

Of the Trinity 'Abdu'l-Bahá says: 'That Lordly Reality admits of no division; for division and multiplicity are properties of creatures . . . The Divine Reality is sanctified from singleness, then how much more from plurality. . . . All that is mentioned of the Manifestations and Dawning-places of God signifies the divine reflection, and not a descent into the conditions of existence.'[35]

Sin and redemption

The Christology of the Church and the teachings of Bahá'u'lláh about Christ's mission are on essential questions irreconcilable. But if we follow analytical theological research over the last decades, we may register the amazing fact that on many questions it is bringing results irreconcilable with the Church's teaching positions but remarkably in accord with the teachings of the Bahá'í Faith.

This unconscious approach may be illustrated in regard to the doctrine of original sin. The central importance accorded to Jesus Christ by both Protestant and Catholic Churches arises from the supposition that Adam and Eve became sinful in Paradise (where they could not distinguish between good and evil) by eating from the 'Tree of Knowledge' against God's will. This caused a deep gulf to open between God and man, which was bridged only by the crucifixion of Christ, the 'Son of God', and by his blood. Baptism brings man into the community of Christ and allows him to participate in redemption. Without wishing to hurt the feelings of devout Christians, I would venture a few critical remarks on this point.

(1) The Gospels offer no indication that Christ saw his mission as having any connection with the Fall in Paradise. The theologian Gross writes: 'Nowhere in the Synoptic Gospels does Jesus attribute man's sin and misery to original sin, even less to inherited sin. The biblical account of the Fall clearly did not have for him the fundamental significance accorded to it by Paul and the Church.'[36]

(2) It is not only Bahá'ís, Muslims and Jews—all of whom also count the Old Testament among the Holy Scriptures—who infer no absolute and eternal sin from the story of Adam and Eve in Paradise; the Christians themselves are divided on this question. Most of the Eastern churches have no definite doctrine of original sin; and in the last century the doctrine was categorically rejected by an Abyssinian theological school. The earlier Church Fathers even declared expressly that children were born without sin. As to the Reformers, while Luther was an extreme believer in original sin, Zwingli rejected it as not in accordance with the Gospels. Many scholars today see Augustine as the actual founder of the dogma.[37] Even Paul, who paved the way for this idea, reports that within the community at Corinth children of Christian parents were not baptized. The Ebionites, who were accused by the Church of relapsing into Judaism, but who were in fact carrying on the tradition of the original Christian community (as the researches of the German religious historian H. J. Schoeps have shown), did not con-

nect the crucifixion with 'atonement' for sin. Original sin in its present sense and content did not become dogma until the sixteenth century.

(3) As to the development of the doctrine of original sin, we must bear in mind that the climate of ideas in ancient times was different and that people then thought in different categories from people in the twentieth century. The thinking of those days, which has come down to us in parables, took for granted irrational elements, such as miracles. As the theologian Trede writes in this connection: 'One lived thinking and believing in a world of miracles, as a fish in water.'[38] Most of the miracles attributed to Jesus in the Gospels can also be found in pre-Christian literature. The masses in any religion are more impressed by magic and ideas of the hereafter than by the spiritual character, the ethic; they want something to happen *for* them, not *through* them.

The orthodox Christian may be surprised to hear that almost everything reported about the circumstances and events of Jesus's life is paralleled in the accounts of Buddha, Zoroaster, Hercules, Dionysus, Aesculapius, the Essenes' 'Teacher of Righteousness', Attis, Osiris, and Adonis. The Emperor cult, the Mithraic cult, and the Gnostics also have striking characteristics in common with the Christian idea of Christ. The account of the resurrection of the gods Attis and Osiris shows a great resemblance even in externals to that of Christ's resurrection. Bel-Marduk, Babylon's most revered deity, is captured, cross-examined, condemned and put to death alongside a criminal, while another criminal is released. Then Marduk goes down to hell and rescues the prisoners. The theologian Carl Schneider writes: 'Christianity has been most deeply influenced, above all by two great creations from Greek mythology, the myth of the man who becomes a god, who suffers with man and dies; and the myth of the imprisoned soul and its liberation by a divine redeemer.'[39]

The doctrine of the divine incarnation and of God's appearance in human form was so widespread in those days that the inhabitants of Lystra, after seeing the miracles of Paul and Barnabas, called out, 'The gods are come down to us in the likeness of men. And they called Barnabas, Jupiter; and Paul, Mercurius, because he was the chief speaker.'[40] Nor were the ancients unfamiliar with the idea that reconciliation with God or gods could be achieved through the killing and sacrificing of human beings. Many races of the Mediterranean, such as the Canaanites, Moabites and Carthaginians, sacrificed children—criminals later took the place of children—thereby to reconcile themselves with God. The Passover lamb was a substitute for the sacrifice of the first-born. Even in our own time we can still find individuals and people who believe that God or gods can be appeased only by blood. In 1933 a sect in the United States killed two people sacrificially. In Chile in 1960 Red Indians sacrificed two people of their own tribe to the gods. In India a mother killed her four-year-old daughter to appease the anger of a deity.

It is striking that the Gospel accounts, if regarded as historical documents, show marked inconsistencies in all questions concerning the life of Jesus and above all his death and resurrection. It is not very surprising, therefore, that critical theological research indicates as especially dubious the parts of the Gospels which show Christ as risen from the dead and as the redeemer of original sin in the sense of the official Creed. Many theologians even want the Creed expurgated and re-worded.

(4) Many theologians admit that the apostle Paul gave the Christian religion a different form from that intended by

its founder. Indeed, Goethe remarked that Paul wrote things which the whole Christian church still does not understand. More recently Albert Schweitzer commented: 'So far as possible he [Paul] avoids quoting anything from the preaching of Jesus, or, indeed, mentioning it at all. If we had been dependent on him for our knowledge, we should not have known that Jesus spoke in parables, preached the Sermon on the Mount, or taught His disciples the Lord's Prayer. Paul even fails to mention sayings of Jesus in connections where they lay directly to his hand.'[41]

Wilhelm Nestle writes: 'Christianity is the religion founded by Paul which replaces the Gospel of Jesus by a gospel about Jesus.'[42] And, according to the theologian H. J. Schoeps, Paul 'misunderstood everything right from the start.'[43] The effect of this false assessment was that, in contrast to all other historical religions, in Christianity a person became the centre rather than the teachings. Karl-Heinz Deschner writes: 'Jesus's ethic of love, which is central to his preaching, was made secondary by the Church (following Paul); and the Church gave pride of place not to his faith but to a faith *in him* which he had not preached. Metaphysics instead of ethic, faith instead of love, Christology instead of the Sermon on the Mount . . . dogma became more important than ethics, the right creed rather than right action.'[44]

(5) If we now ask how it was possible for such distortions to have developed in Christianity, I would point out that the adherents of every religion—except the Bahá'ís*—have

---

* The Bahá'ís, however, are not guilty of making eternal truth relative. Their attitude towards the claim to finality and uniqueness is determined by the basic unity of the Manifestations of God, that they belong to the Kingdom of Revelation, and also by the progressive Revelation of God as conditioned by space and time. For the duration of a Manifestation's mission (in the case of Bahá'u'lláh, by his own testimony, not less than a thousand years), his teachings and commandments have

SIN AND REDEMPTION

claimed finality for their faith, which amounts to making the special features of each Revelation of God exclusive, unsurpassable and unalterable. The claim to uniqueness is something which Zoroastrians, Jews and Muslims all take for granted, though with different justifications in each case. In Islám, for instance, the justification centres on the verses in the Qur'án calling Muḥammad the 'seal of the prophets', or on the concept that the Qur'án is the embodiment of revelation.

The time span in which Jesus was able to work and teach was very short, and even in that span he was continually subject to persecutions, which only ended with his early death. The crucifixion took his disciples completely by surprise. They became despondent, and dispersed. Christ's teachings were above all spiritual and less inclined towards commandments and prohibitions. So it was much harder for the Christians to find a doctrinal pivot for the claim of their faith to finality and uniqueness, which could meet the challenge of argument with heretics. The signs and phenomena, however, accompanying the earthly life of Jesus, from his birth to the crucifixion, were so very different from the course of an ordinary man's life that an irresistible temptation arose to give an absolute character to his person

---

absolute validity. They are absolute for man because unalterable by him. They are relative because God cannot be bound by men to His own legislation. In the Qur'án we find these important words rejecting a claim to finality for the teachings of Moses and the religious ideas of the Jews: ' "The hand of God," say the Jews, "is chained up". Their own hands shall be chained up. . . . Nay! outstretched are both His hands! At His own pleasure does He bestow gifts . . .' (Súrih v, 69). The same point is made in the words of Christ, 'The wind bloweth where it listeth' (John iii, 8) and the words of Bahá'u'lláh, 'He doth what He pleaseth. He chooseth; and none may question His choice.' (*Gleanings from the Writings of Bahá'u'lláh*, CLV.)

and the circumstances of his life. In fact it is not the authority and superiority inherent in Christ's Word which has developed into the centre of the faith, but his person and the story of his earthly life.

(6) It seems strange that today, in this scientific age, we should attribute symbolic meaning to the creation of Adam from dust, the entire story of the Creation, the Garden of Eden, and give it all an allegorical interpretation, with the single exception of the Fall.

The idea of absolute sin is unknown to the Bahá'ís. 'Abdu'l-Bahá says: 'All sin comes from the demands of nature, and these demands, which arise from the physical qualities, are not sins with respect to the animals, while for man they are sin. The animal is the source of imperfections, such as anger, sensuality, jealousy, avarice, cruelty, pride: all these defects are found in animals, but do not constitute sins. But in man they are sins.'[45] And he further states: 'The physical nature is inherited from Adam, and the spiritual nature is inherited from the Reality of the Word of God, which is the spirituality of Christ. The physical nature is born of Adam, but the spiritual nature is born from the bounty of the Holy Spirit; the first is the source of all imperfection, the second is the source of all perfection. The Christ sacrified himself so that men might be freed from the imperfections of the physical nature, and might become possessed of the virtues of the spiritual nature.'[46]

The commandments and teachings in every revelation set a standard of goodness; to depart from them is sin. This means that good and evil are not fixed in their value once for all, but are themselves subject to development. For instance, everything which is opposed today to the unity of mankind and world peace is 'sin' in the eyes of the Bahá'ís.

SIN AND REDEMPTION

The events in the life of Jesus may give us cause for reflection and reverence, but Christ's spiritual greatness towers high above these features. That is why the Cross is a sacred symbol for the Bahá'ís but they do not worship it. The Messenger of God is from the outset exalted above the limitations of the human station. For the Bahá'ís, it would make no difference to the station of Christ, as Manifestation of God, if he had not been crucified but had departed from this world by stoning or a normal death. If anyone tries to prove the uniqueness of such a Messenger of God by pointing to particular details in his life, the objection can rightly be made that there is something unique about everything in creation. No two people or their fates, no two seeds or even two atoms, are absolutely the same. If, for instance, Christ's greatness were derived from the manner of his birth, then Adam would be still greater ('Abdu'l-Bahá observes), because he had neither mother nor father.[47]

For the Bahá'ís, hell signifies remoteness from God, and heaven, nearness to Him. They could never accept the logic of the doctrine of original sin, which would make all men sinners, including saints and prophets, Abraham, Moses and John the Baptist, and would mean that the Messengers of God before Jesus did not really possess at all the divine authority which brings salvation. The Bahá'ís cannot conceive of a Deity who prescribes for man an unconditional love of neighbour and enemy, but who is Himself unable to forgive unless He has had 'satisfaction' (along the lines of Roman law) through the blood of His son. The insights of earlier great spirits like Goethe, Nietzsche and Schopenhauer seem to be gradually becoming common property. The Catholic theologian Thomas Sartory writes: 'So a theology of justification may well seem "biblical" . . . and yet not be. This applies when such a theology (unconsciously) uses biblical terms in a framework of ideas different from the biblical framework.'[48]

According to Bahá'u'lláh, recognition of the divine Manifestation and obedience to his teachings and commandments form the two main duties of man in this world. The paths travelled by the faithful soul on the way to its goal, nearness to God, have been described by Bahá'u'lláh in two mystical writings, *The Seven Valleys* and *The Four Valleys*. Finally, we may also quote his words regarding the Bahá'í attitude to Christ's crucifixion and miracles:

'Know thou that when the Son of Man yielded up His breath to God, the whole creation wept with a great weeping. By sacrificing Himself, however, a fresh capacity was infused into all created things. Its evidences, as witnessed in all the peoples of the earth, are now manifest before thee. The deepest wisdom which the sages have uttered, the profoundest learning which any mind hath unfolded, the arts which the ablest hands have produced, the influence exerted by the most potent of rulers, are but manifestations of the quickening power released by His transcendent, His all-pervasive, and resplendent Spirit.

'We testify that when He came into the world, He shed the splendour of His glory upon all created things. Through Him the leper recovered from the leprosy of perversity and ignorance. Through Him, the unchaste and wayward were healed. Through His power, born of Almighty God, the eyes of the blind were opened, and the soul of the sinner sanctified.

'Leprosy may be interpreted as any veil that interveneth between man and the recognition of the Lord, his God. Whoso alloweth himself to be shut out from Him is indeed a leper, who shall not be remembered in the Kingdom of God, the Mighty, the All-Praised. We bear witness that through the power of the Word of God every leper was cleansed, every sickness was healed, every human infirmity was banished. He it is Who purified the world. Blessed is the man who, with a face beaming with light, hath turned towards Him.'[49]

IX

THE NEW HEAVEN

'O Pope! Rend the veils asunder. He Who is the Lord of Lords is come overshadowed with clouds, and the decree hath been fulfilled by God . . . Dwellest thou in palaces whilst He Who is the King of Revelation liveth in the most desolate of abodes? Leave them unto such as desire them, and set thy face with joy and delight towards the Kingdom . . . Arise in the name of thy Lord, the God of Mercy, amidst the peoples of the earth, and seize thou the Cup of Life with the hands of confidence, and first drink thou therefrom, and proffer it then to such as turn towards it amongst the peoples of all faiths . . .

'Call thou to remembrance Him Who was the Spirit [Jesus], Who, when He came, the most learned of His age pronounced judgment against Him in His own country, whilst he who was only a fisherman believed in Him.'[1]

Bahá'u'lláh

The most important message of the Gospels

IF we ask which is the most important message in the Gospels and the one most often referred to, we come upon many passages and many parables announcing the kingdom of God and the judgment it entails (the 'Last Judgment'). The concept 'kingdom of God' comes fourteen times in Mark, thirty times in Luke and somewhat more often in Matthew, although Matthew nearly always uses the expression 'kingdom of heaven'. The word 'church', however—the foundation of the Christian hierarchy—appears only twice in all the Gospels together.

Because of the glad tidings that the kingdom of God is near, serious theologians and philosophers have concluded, wrongly in my view, that in this context Jesus Christ himself erred. Jaspers, for instance, says that the eschatological expectation (of the Last Judgment) was an error in terms of cosmic knowledge. Heiler writes that no one disputes today that Jesus was firmly convinced of the imminence of the Day of Judgment and the consummation of the world—although in fact there *are* today scholars who dispute this. According to Bultmann, no proof is needed to show that Jesus was mistaken in expecting the end of the world to be near.

Doubtless the apostles and the original Christian community expected it from one day to the next. This is shown by the letters of Peter, Paul and James, the Revelation of John and the literature of the Church Fathers, and also by the way of life of the first Christians. Expectation of the Messiah, connected with the certainty of an apocalyptic end, has been a feature of the entire history of Christendom. The pealing of the Church bells was, and is, a reminder to believers, day and night, that the end may be at hand; Christians should prepare themselves for the Lord's coming at any moment. Unfortunately the sense of the warning has been lost in our day. The bells peal to celebrate a joyful event or a sad one, but never to remind us that the Lord may appear at any moment like a 'thief in the night'. It was far otherwise in the days of the disciples and the first Christians. They had been living with the Messianic expectation and had drawn their hope from it. Most scholars today agree that Jesus's disciples confidently expected that his second coming was near and would coincide with the virtual end of time. Later, however, when the Christians won influence and power, so that it was an advantage and not a drawback to be a Christian, there were mixed feelings in contemplating the end of the world.

Thus the Church Fathers in the fourth century prayed: 'May this never be fulfilled in our day! For terrible is the Lord's descent to earth.'[2] Scholars today also see the Messianic expectation as a reason why the Gospels were composed so late. Christ's immediate circle, who after his death were daily reckoning on the end of the world, thought it superfluous to put down anything for posterity.

The idea of the return is of the utmost importance in Judaism, Islám and the other great religions as well as in Christianity. Many devout Jews today do not recognize the State of Israel, opposing its claim to be a state, because they connect its founding with their Messianic expectation; the Jewish state, they believe, will not be established until the expected Messiah has come. In the Qur'án the ideas of 'Judgment' and 'Last Days' are to be found in many Súrihs, especially the final ones, which are devoted exclusively to this theme, as in Súrih XCIX:

> In the Name of God, the Compassionate, the Merciful
> When the Earth with her quaking shall quake
> And the Earth shall cast forth her burdens . . .
> On that day shall men come forward in throngs to behold their works,
> And whosoever shall have wrought an atom's weight of good shall behold it,
> And whosoever shall have wrought an atom's weight of evil shall behold it.

Much in the Qur'án is similar to Matthew's Gospel, where the darkening of the sun and moon is reported and 'the stars shall fall from heaven'; '. . . then shall all the tribes of the earth mourn, and they shall see the Son of man coming on the clouds of heaven with power and great glory. And he shall send his angels with a great sound of a trumpet...'[3] But these days are accompanied by the appearance of many false prophets, who appear in sheep's clothing and yet are ravening wolves.

The false prophets

The idea of the false prophet has played a big part in Christianity in the fight against other religions. In the past especially, the Christian clergy on the whole have considered any genuine discussion with other religions (whose founders they called 'false prophets') to be superfluous or even harmful, since their followers might well be seduced and corrupted by contact with them. The Bahá'ís believe that the negative development of Christianity is partly due to the activities of the real 'false prophets'—narrow-minded and intolerant clergy and theologians.

It seems important, indeed, to remember that the word 'prophet' is used in the Gospels especially for inspired teachers working within the Christian community, as distinct from the apostles who were often preaching on their journeys and were active in the mission field. In the old Church hierarchy the prophets were subordinate to the apostles, a title not confined just to the twelve chosen by Christ.

The order of precedence comes out clearly in I Corinthians xii, 28–31: 'And God hath set some in the church, first apostles, secondarily prophets, thirdly teachers, after that miracles, then gifts of healings, helps, governments, diversities of tongues. Are all apostles? are all prophets? are all teachers? are all workers of miracles? Have all the gifts of healing? do all speak with tongues? do all interpret? But covet earnestly the best gifts...' In I Corinthians xiv, 28–9, we read: 'But if there be no interpreter, let him keep silence in the church; and let him speak to himself, and to God. Let the prophets speak two or three, and let the other judge.' What a large number of prophets there must have been in a single church, if only two or three were told they might speak.

So is it not fair to consider as 'false prophets' the authoritative priests and theologians who gave Christianity a different direction and a different content from what was intended by the Founder of this religion? I think it *is* fair, on the basis of Christ's reference to the countless schisms and sects of the future—which would tear Christianity to pieces by the time of the Lord's return: 'And then if any man shall say to you, Lo, here is Christ; or, lo, he is there; believe him not: . . .'[4] The false prophets have on their conscience the leading astray of countless Christians who followed them. It is a dismaying thought that most Christians, in fact almost all, are prevented by these perversions from finding their way to the original message in matters of faith. This, however, has been the fate of all the historic religions and their followers.

The Messianic expectation

The Messianic expectation reached its peak in the last century. Everywhere—in other religions too besides Christianity—the Lord's imminent coming was hoped for. In America various adventist movements arose, which even gave the exact date of the Second Coming, according to their interpretation of the Scriptures, as the year 1844.*
There were Wolff in Asia, Edward Irving in Scotland, Davis

---

* Among the adventist movements still very active today are Catholic-Apostolic Communities, Seventh Day Adventists, Jehovah's Witnesses, the Church of the Kingdom of God, the Philadelphia Movement, the Brotherhood of the Kingdom of Jesus Christ; and also the Shaykhís, a sect of the Shí'ih Muslims.

in South Carolina, William Miller in Pennsylvania, to mention only a few; while from Württemberg in Germany many expectant folk migrated to Palestine and settled on the slopes of Mount Carmel. They were all hoping for the Lord to appear soon. Similar movements grew up in Judaism and more especially in Islám, where religious schools prepared many for the coming of the Expected One.

What an irony of fate! For many centuries Christendom has expected the Lord's return and prophesied in connection with it the destruction of the world. The rationalists and scientists considered all this superstitious nonsense and derided those who believed it. Today the situation is exactly reversed. The scientists and social historians prophesy no happy future for humanity. Lewis Mumford writes that rationally speaking the chances of a 'world-transforming miracle' occurring are less than one in a million: by a miracle in this context he means the intervention of an outstanding personality or a vigilant group which at the right moment, the right place and with the right ideas, should gain an influence over the course of events and preserve humanity from complete destruction. If it came to a bet, Mumford continues, it would be safer for one to gamble on an imminent disaster of 'planetary dimensions'.[5] Although Christian theologians have predicted an apocalyptic end for nearly two thousand years, many present-day theologians deny this belief (as pointed out above). Others dismiss the idea of the Second Coming as unrealistic, so that we in our time and with our consciousness do not need to come to grips with it.

Bahá'u'lláh's claim

In studying Bahá'u'lláh's writings we shall continually come upon his unmistakable claim to be Christ returned.

Addressing himself to the Christian clergy, he writes: 'O concourse of priests! . . . It behooveth you, in this day, to proclaim aloud the Most Great Name among the nations. Prefer ye to be silent, whilst every stone and every tree shouteth aloud: "The Lord is come in His great glory!" . . . Let the Breeze of God awaken you. . . .' And again: 'The Day of Reckoning hath appeared, the Day whereon He Who was in heaven hath come. He, verily, is the One Whom ye were promised in the Books of God, the Holy, the Almighty, the All-Praised. How long will ye wander in the wilderness of heedlessness and superstition? . . .'[6]

This claim is so great and important that any serious Christian must think hard about it. He may ask: How is Bahá'u'lláh to be understood as Christ returned? How does this fit in with the prophecies of the Old and New Testaments and the signs which are supposed to accompany Christ's Second Coming? I have already mentioned man's inability to perceive supernatural truths directly and his dependence on the language of images, on metaphors and similes which tell him of the supernatural world and the hereafter. Every Christian has certain ideas that he connects with Christ's return. But in the Gospels the descriptions of how this will take place and of the signs accompanying it do not agree with each other.

In Matthew there is a detailed description, quoted above, of how the 'Son of man' will come 'in the clouds of heaven with power and great glory'.[7] Elsewhere, however, the return is compared to the coming of a 'thief in the night'.[8] In Luke we read: '. . . that day [will] come upon you unawares. For as a snare shall it come on all them that dwell on the face of the whole earth.'[9] And also: 'The kingdom of God cometh not with observation . . .'[10] Whereas Matthew again says: 'For as the lightning cometh out of the east, and shineth even unto the west; so shall also the coming of the Son of man be.'[11]

The images for Christ's return range, then, from the meteor-like lightning to the thief in the night. On the one hand Christ comes from heaven absolutely visible and incarnate; on the other the kingdom of God is not to be observed externally and objectively. These conflicting statements have naturally led to the most varied interpretations. There are Christians who expect a return in the visible world and in human form. Others think the return is to be understood spiritually, and they interpret it as Christ's presence in the community. Still others refer the return, which in their view has already taken place, to the phenomena which the disciples experienced at Whitsun. The large number of eschatological and apocalyptic statements in the Bible also leads Christians of various denominations and sects to an abundance of ideas of the return which are mutually contradictory. No wonder the second plenary session of the World Council of Churches (at Evanston in 1954) could not agree on this question.

I think it is important to remember that all these divergent ideas and opinions provide no standard for recognizing the true significance of Christ's return. They have as little importance for the appreciation of Jesus's mission as did the interpretations of the Old Testament by the Jews. 'The spirit bloweth where it listeth', and a new outpouring of divine truth cannot be predicted and recognized by theological systems, for the Messenger of God sits, as Bahá'u'lláh says, on the throne of 'He, verily, doeth whatsoever He willeth.'[12] Christ had already warned against pouring new wine into old bottles. The criterion is and will remain the living Word of God. It is not we who possess a standard by which to test a Messenger; it is he who tests us.

When such a tremendous claim as Bahá'u'lláh's is made on us, we must bear in mind that we are the tested and can at most be seekers. We ourselves and the theologians should be far humbler on essential questions.

The concept of 'heaven'

To realize the inadequacy of theology when it meets the new living Word of God, we need only follow the way the concept of 'heaven' has changed its meaning in the course of history. In the Middle Ages people knew what they meant by heaven. The throne of God was there, and on His right hand Jesus Christ reigned, with the angels hovering around them. This idea fitted in well with the mediaeval expectation of Christ's Second Coming: in the hour of fulfilment he was to come down to earth, accompanied by angels. The people who travelled from Württemberg to the Holy Land in the middle of the nineteenth century to witness Christ's return, took telescopes with them. This Christian cosmology has been destroyed by the progress of science. Modern theologians understand by heaven not a place but a condition.

This raises two questions:

(1) If heaven is a condition, not a place, how is Mary's bodily assumption to heaven to be understood? What does the word 'bodily' mean here? Doubtless we are concerned with two different planes, which have nothing to do with each other, just as in mathematics you cannot add pounds to inches.

(2) If heaven is a condition, not a place, what about the other parallel conceptions and the religious language of the New Testament? What about the earth as the counterpart to heaven? What about the sun, moon, stars and clouds? Are these references to be understood literally, although heaven is not a place?

As long ago as 1925 Professor Whitehead wrote: 'Religion is tending to degenerate into a decent formula wherewith to embellish a comfortable life . . . for over two centuries religion has been on the defensive and on a weak defensive. The period has been one of unprecedented intellectual progress. In this way a series of novel situations have been produced for thought. Each such occasion has found the religious thinkers unprepared. Something, which has been proclaimed to be vital, has finally, after struggle, distress, and anathema, been modified and otherwise interpreted. The next generation of religious apologists then congratulates the religious world on the deeper insight which has been gained. The result of the continued repetition of this undignified retreat, during many generations, has at last almost entirely destroyed the intellectual authority of religious thinkers. Consider this contrast: when Darwin or Einstein proclaims theories which modify our ideas, it is a triumph for science. We do not go about saying that there is another defeat for science, because its old ideas have been abandoned. We know that another step of scientific insight has been gained.'[13]

That Christ used the term 'heaven' in a way which precludes a literal explanation can be seen from the fact that before his crucifixion he said: 'For I came down from heaven, not to do mine own will, but the will of him that sent me';[14] '. . . no man hath ascended up to heaven, but he that came down from heaven, even the Son of man which is in heaven.'[15]

So he declared not only that he was going to heaven but also that he had come from heaven, although he was born of Mary and was also *in* heaven at the point in time when he was talking to his disciples and travelling with them. If the concept of 'heaven' can thus be understood only in a symbolic sense, what makes Christians so certain that the other images, like sun, moon and stars, used in connection with the promise of a Second Coming, are only to be interpreted in their literal meaning? Should Christians not let their own history serve as a warning?

In Isaiah xl, 3–5, it is said: 'The voice of him that crieth in the wilderness, Prepare ye the way of the LORD, make straight in the desert a highway for our God. Every valley shall be exalted, and every mountain and hill shall be made low: and the crooked shall be made straight, and the rough places plain: And the glory of the LORD shall be revealed, and all flesh shall see it together: for the mouth of the LORD hath spoken it.'

On the appearance of Christ it became evident that this prophecy, to which John the Baptist also referred,[16] was not fully realized: the 'glory of the Lord' was not seen by all 'flesh', nor were the hills made low or the valleys exalted. Christ appeared in such a way that the Jews and the Pharisees could ask, 'Can there any good thing come out of Nazareth?'[17] Many signs which Christians expect at Christ's Second Coming were expected by the Jews at the coming of the Messiah according to *their* prophecies—for instance, that he would come surrounded by angels, would execute judgment and bring all Israel's dead back to life. That such expectations had no literal fulfilment at the coming of John the Baptist and Jesus should make Christians rather cautious in their various ideas about the Second Coming.

In one of his most important writings, *The Book of Certitude**, Bahá'u'lláh indicated the basis on which the various religions and denominations can become reconciled to each other. He explained the significance of the symbolic terms used in the Holy Scriptures: 'heaven' is the will of God, the divine Revelation; the 'clouds' are the obstacles

* *Kitáb-i-Íqán.*

hindering people from recognizing and accepting the Revealer. Thus, the fact that the Messengers of God come to us in the human 'temple', that is, in human form (as a carpenter's son, a merchant, a camel-driver), is to be considered as an obstacle (cloud) to their recognition. By 'sun' and 'moon' we understand the teachings and the divine laws. The Messenger of God himself is also called 'Sun' in the Scriptures—and these, of course, are not the only meanings for the words 'heaven', 'sun', 'moon', 'clouds', etc.[18] Life and death are to be understood spiritually, as in Christ's words, 'let the dead bury their dead'.[19]

Bahá'u'lláh writes: 'You will readily recognize that the terms sovereignty, wealth, life, death, judgment and resurrection, spoken of by the scriptures of old, are not what this generation hath conceived and vainly imagined. Nay, by sovereignty is meant that sovereignty which in every dispensation resideth within, and is exercised by, the person of the Manifestation, the Day-star of Truth. That sovereignty is the spiritual ascendancy which He exerciseth to the fullest degree over all that is in heaven and on earth, and which in due time revealeth itself to the world in direct proportion to its capacity and spiritual receptiveness.'[20]

There is no point in trying to understand literally and word for word all these biblical passages and prophecies. It would be like sitting in a theatre watching some great and perhaps terrifying spectacle without realizing its religious significance. Rúḥu'lláh Varqá, a young Bahá'í martyred in Ṭihrán with his father at the age of thirteen, was once asked what he would do if a figure such as that described in the New Testament should come down from heaven accompanied by angels. He was then eleven, and without hesitation answered, showing the insignificance of any outward circumstances compared with the spiritual supremacy of the divine Manifestation: 'I would hurry over and deliver Bahá'u'lláh's Message to him.'

Bahá'u'lláh: The Promised One of all religions

Bahá'u'lláh, by his own testimony, is the Promised One of all religions: 'The All-Merciful is come invested with undoubted sovereignty. The Balance hath been appointed, and all them that dwell on earth have been gathered together. The Trumpet hath been blown, and lo, all eyes have stared up with terror, and the hearts of all who are in the heavens and on the earth have trembled, except them whom the breath of the verses of God hath quickened, and who have detached themselves from all things. . . .

'. . . We see the people laid low, awed with the dread of thy Lord, the Almighty, the Most Powerful. The Crier hath cried out, and men have been torn away, so great hath been the fury of His wrath. The people of the left hand sigh and bemoan. The people of the right abide in noble habitations: they quaff the Wine that is life indeed, from the hands of the All-Merciful, and are, verily, the blissful.

'The earth hath been shaken, and the mountains have passed away, and the angels have appeared, rank on rank, before Us. Most of the people are bewildered in their drunkenness and wear on their faces the evidences of anger. . . . We point out to them those that led them astray. They see them, and yet recognize them not. Their eyes are drunken . . .

'. . . The shout hath been raised, and the people have come forth from their graves, and arising are gazing around them. Some have made haste to attain the court of the God of Mercy, others have fallen down on their faces in the fire of Hell, while still others are lost in bewilderment. The verses of God have been revealed, and yet they have turned away from them. . . . Whether ye rejoice or whether ye burst for fury, the heavens are cleft asunder, and God hath come down, invested with radiant sovereignty. All created things are heard exclaiming: "The Kingdom is God's, the Almighty, the All-Knowing, the All-Wise." '[21]

The expectations of all religions have in the eyes of the Bahá'ís received their fulfilment in Bahá'u'lláh. Shoghi Effendi writes:

'To Him Isaiah, the greatest of the Jewish prophets, had alluded as the *"Glory of the Lord"*, the *"Everlasting Father"*, the *"Prince of Peace"*, the *"Wonderful"*, the *"Counsellor"*, the *"Rod come forth out of the stem of Jesse"* and the *"Branch grown out of His roots"*, Who *"shall be established upon the throne of David"*, Who *"will come with strong hand"*, Who *"shall judge among the nations"* . . .

'To His Dispensation the sacred books of the followers of Zoroaster had referred as that in which the sun must needs be brought to a standstill for no less than one whole month.* To Him Zoroaster must have alluded when, according to tradition, He foretold that a period of three thousand years of conflict and contention must needs precede the advent of the World-Saviour, Sháh-Bahrám, Who would triumph over Ahriman and usher in an era of blessedness and peace.

'He alone is meant by the prophecy attributed to Gautama Buddha Himself, that *"a Buddha named Maitreye, the Buddha of universal fellowship"* should, in the fullness of time, arise and reveal *"His boundless glory"*. To Him the Bhagavad-Gita of the Hindus had referred as the *"Most Great Spirit"*, the *"Tenth Avatar"*, the *"Immaculate Manifestation of Krishna"*. . . .

'To Him Muḥammad . . . had alluded in His Book as the

* This marks the specially powerful outpouring of the 'Sun of Truth'. (H.S.)

"*Great Announcement*", and declared His Day to be the Day whereon "*God*" will "*come down*" "*overshadowed with clouds*", the Day whereon "*thy Lord shall come and the angels rank on rank*", and "*The Spirit shall arise and the angels shall be ranged in order*". His advent He, in that Book, in a súrih said to have been termed by Him "*the heart of the Qur'án*", had foreshadowed as that of the "*third*" Messenger, sent down to "*strengthen*" the two who preceded Him. . . .'

As to the expectations contained in the New Testament, Shoghi Effendi states:

'To Him the Author of the Apocalypse had alluded as the "*Glory of God*",* as "*Alpha and Omega*", "*the Beginning and the End*", "*the First and the Last*". Identifying His Revelation with the "*third woe*", he, moreover, had extolled His Law as "*a new heaven and a new earth*", as the "*Tabernacle of God*", as the "*Holy City*", as the "*New Jerusalem, coming down from God out of heaven . . .*" '

And he reminds us of the remarkable promises given by Christ to his loyal followers:

'To Him Jesus Christ had referred as . . . the "*Comforter*" Who will "*reprove the world of sin, and of righteousness, and of judgment*", as the "*Spirit of Truth*" Who "*will guide you into all truth*", Who "*shall not speak of Himself, but whatsoever He shall hear, that shall He speak*", as the "*Lord of the Vineyard*", and as the "*Son of Man*" Who "*shall come in the glory of His Father*" "*in the clouds of heaven with power and great glory*", with "*all the holy angels*" about Him, and "*all nations*" gathered before His throne.'[22]

William Sears, an American Bahá'í, investigated hundreds of biblical passages and the prophecies contained in them, and showed how they all refer to Bahá'u'lláh's mission.[23]

* This is the meaning of 'Bahá'u'lláh'. (H.S.)

Every Messenger of God bears within himself the proof of his own truth. The promises and prophecies of earlier religions, however detailed and accurate, have really no evidential value for the Bahá'ís. I have referred to them, therefore, not as proofs but rather to stimulate reflection.

Some people are very disappointed by the great religions in their present form and the unhappy situation of their representatives. They think that in an enlightened but disenchanted world a new religion of revelation has no prospects, since the conditions and premises from which religions formerly developed no longer exist today. The historical religions succeeded, such people maintain, because particular personalities favoured by circumstance managed to convert the ignorant masses to their beliefs; but in our enlightened age not only must the power of past religions dwindle, no new religion can possibly emerge.

These sceptics are clearly refuted by the emergence and swift spread of the Bahá'í Faith. Our age, indeed, is the first to provide the conditions for the development of a truly universal religion. Not that the Bahá'ís understand their religion as compelling men to adopt particular rules and laws; they see it rather, in 'Abdu'l-Bahá's definition of religion and truth, as 'the essential connection which proceeds from the realities of things'.[24] A doctor is not using force when he prescribes for a patient a particular remedy or treatment; it is a 'natural' necessity for the patient's healing and well-being. In exactly the same way the ordinances and commandments of a Manifestation of God—the Divine Physician—are necessary teachings related to the 'natural' needs of humanity.

Anyone following the growth of the Bahá'í Faith in the last decades will find that it appeals equally to adherents of all religions and denominations. It is clear that in this faith all peoples, to whatever race, nation or religion they may belong, start on the same terms. It is hard to say whether Catholics or Protestants, Africans or Asians, are adopting the Bahá'í Faith in larger numbers.

Rationalists have never predicted much future for a new religion. How contemptuously the Sassanid kings dismissed Muḥammad and his teachings! How many Romans in about A.D. 150 foresaw that Christianity would triumph and that their Empire would fall? But religion as 'the essential connection which proceeds from the realities of things' sees God's Messenger as a perfect teacher or doctor who by his appearance and his creative force, his teachings and laws, helps men to overcome their situation, so apparently hopeless and chaotic. He is the point of crystallization for a new stage of development. His authority unites the divided and contending forces. He is like a permanent magnet which magnetizes the iron of men's hearts; the purer their hearts, the more easily can he change them also into magnets, which in turn will influence and shape their environment. In human history the rise of a religion has always been bound up with the rise of a civilization. If a piece of iron loses its relation to the permanent magnet, its own magnetism will gradually disappear.

History teaches us that science and rationalist philosophy cannot replace the unifying power and authority of a Manifestation of God. In our time, particularly, it is very clearly brought home to us how much the lack of a universally recognized authority is responsible for man's chaotic situation. Technologists may seize every opportunity to rationalize their efforts; nevertheless in the social field, for lack of a recognized authority, forces are wasted or even mobilized in many cases to the detriment of mankind. We have today neither a universal language, an essential if people all over the world are to understand each other, nor international standards in weights and measures, currency and law. There is no common economic conception for the whole world. There is still not enough international exchange of the results of research, so that vast sums of money are spent by different countries on similar research projects. The losses thus incurred by mankind can scarcely be expressed in figures; but the picture would change at once if an impartial universal authority were recognized. The Bahá'ís are certain that such an authority, which can unite the opposed sections of humanity, can only be an authority founded on the guidance of God.

A new vision must be brought to mankind, a deeper understanding of the essential nature of man and the world, which at the same time creates a more living relationship to the divine. So I would ask critics to observe, if not with love, at least without hatred, the activities of those who have been stirred by Bahá'u'lláh's Revelation, and not to lose sight of its influence on our age. Whereas the long time-span separating us from earlier Messengers of God means that we cannot now ascertain exactly the facts concerning their existence on earth and confirm through them the authentic Word of God, we are in a position to follow accurately the life and work of Bahá'u'lláh in all its phases through the written testimonies at our disposal. These include the equivalent of a hundred volumes of Bahá'u'lláh's authentic writings, which constitute a unique gift in the history of mankind.*

Thus we know that His Revelation was born in Ṭihrán in the darkness of an underground prison, which had formerly

---

* While only a small part of this 'ocean of knowledge' is, as yet, translated into Western languages, already sufficient is available through the translations of Shoghi Effendi to give every student of Bahá'u'lláh's writings a clear and ample understanding of them.

been used as a cistern for public baths. In the darkness of this dungeon, characterized by its stench and intolerable humidity, with a heavy chain round his neck and his feet in fetters, saddened by the martyrdom of the Báb and the deaths of thousands of his most devoted followers, Bahá'u'lláh received the inspiration of the 'Most Great Spirit', as he himself testifies: 'One night, in a dream, these exalted words were heard on every side: "Verily, We shall render Thee victorious by Thyself and by Thy Pen. Grieve Thou not for that which hath befallen Thee, neither be Thou afraid, for Thou art in safety. Ere long will God raise up the treasures of the earth—men who will aid Thee through Thyself and through Thy Name, wherewith God hath revived the hearts of such as have recognized Him".'[25] 'By My Life!' he declares in a Tablet, 'Not of Mine own volition have I revealed Myself, but God, of His own choosing, hath manifested Me.'[26]

In his Tablet addressed to his royal adversary, the ruler of Persia, Náṣiri'd-Dín Sháh, we find the following words of Bahá'u'lláh:

'O King! I was but a man like others, asleep upon My couch, when lo, the breezes of the All-Glorious were wafted over Me, and taught Me the knowledge of all that hath been. This thing is not from Me, but from One Who is Almighty and All-Knowing. And he bade Me lift up My voice between earth and heaven, and for this there befell Me what hath caused the tears of every man of understanding to flow. . . . This is but a leaf which the winds of the will of thy Lord, the Almighty, the All-Praised, have stirred. . . .'[27]

CHRONOLOGICAL TABLE

23 May 1844   The Báb (1819–1850) declares his mission to the first disciple Mullá Ḥusayn (p. 69).

Autumn 1844   The Báb travels to Mecca; the disciples proclaim his mission throughout Persia. Mullá Ḥusayn delivers a Tablet from the Báb to Mírzá Ḥusayn-ʿAlí, later known as Bahá'u'lláh (1817–1892), who accepts the Báb's Revelation.

Summer 1847   The Báb is banished to the fortress of Máh-Kú (p. 72). A meeting planned between him and the Sháh is prevented by the Prime Minister.

July 1848   The Báb is interrogated at Tabríz, in the presence of the heir to the throne, by eminent dignitaries of the Muslim clergy (p. 73).

9 July 1850   The Báb is publicly executed in the barracks square in Tabríz, together with a devoted follower.

August 1852   The peak of the persecutions of the Bábís, following an attempt on the Sháh's life. Thousands of Bábís are martyred, many more imprisoned. Bahá'u'lláh is taken to the Síyáh-Chál (Black Hole), the most notorious prison in Ṭihrán, where he receives the first intimation of his Revelation (pp. 84–5).

January 1853   Bahá'u'lláh is banished with his family to Baghdád.

1854–56	Bahá'u'lláh withdraws to Kurdistán. After two years he returns to Ba<u>gh</u>dád to consolidate the discouraged Bábí community (p. 85).
22 April 1863	Bahá'u'lláh declares his mission in a Ba<u>gh</u>dád garden, proclaiming that he is the Revealer promised by the Báb and by all previous Messengers of God.
3 May 1863	Bahá'u'lláh, with his family and followers, leaves Ba<u>gh</u>dád for Constantinople (Istanbul) as an exile.
December 1863	They are banished from Constantinople to Adrianople.
1867–73	Bahá'u'lláh reveals the *Súriy-i-Mulúk*, a Tablet to the Kings, followed by many Tablets addressed to the secular and religious rulers and authorities of the world.
August 1868	Bahá'u'lláh and his family are banished again, to the penal colony of 'Akká in Palestine.
1870	The fall of Napoleon III, to whom Bahá'u'lláh had sent two warning Tablets. Pope Pius IX loses sovereignty over Rome. (He had also received a warning Tablet from Bahá'u'lláh, urgently commending to him voluntary renunciation of his secular rule.)
1880	Bahá'u'lláh goes to Bahjí, a country house near 'Akká where he spends the evening of his life in relative freedom though still a State prisoner.
29 May 1892	Bahá'u'lláh's death at Bahjí. In his testament he appoints his eldest son 'Abbás Effendi (1844–1921), known as 'Abdu'l-

	Bahá (Servant of Glory), to be the Centre of his Covenant and the authorized interpreter of his words.
23 September 1893	Public reference to the Bahá'í Faith is made in America for the first time.
1902	The building of the first Bahá'í House of Worship is started at 'Ishqábád (Turkmenistan, Russia).
September 1908	Following the outbreak of the Young Turks' Revolution, 'Abdu'l-Bahá is released from incarceration.
1910–11	'Abdu'l-Bahá travels to Egypt, France and England, where he speaks to large audiences, including addresses in London from the pulpit of the City Temple and at St. John's, Westminster.
1912	'Abdu'l-Bahá travels to America, where he gives addresses in various cities and lays the foundation stone of the first House of Worship in the West (at Wilmette, Illinois).
1912–13	'Abdu'l-Bahá again visits Europe, this time including Germany, Hungary and Austria, and warns of the approaching war (p. 90).
1917–25	Fall of the House of Romanov. (Tsar Alexander II was one of the rulers who received Bahá'u'lláh's warning Tablets.) Break-up of the Austro-Hungarian Empire. (Emperor Francis Joseph was censured by Bahá'u'lláh in his 'Most Holy Book' (*Kitáb-i-Aqdas*) for not having investigated his Cause and sought out his presence while visiting the Holy Land.) Fall of the German Imperial House. (After

the fall of Napoleon III, Emperor Wilhelm I was urgently admonished by Bahá'u'lláh. His 'Most Holy Book' contains the words: 'And We hear the lamentations of Berlin, though she be today in conspicuous glory'.) Break-up of the Turkish Empire and abolition of the Sultanate and Caliphate. (Sulṭán ʿAbdu'l-ʿAzíz and his Grand Vazír, ʿÁlí Páshá, received Tablets from Bahá'u'lláh. The chronicler Nabíl records that the latter was so affected on reading the Tablet to the Sulṭán that he turned pale.)

Fall of the Qájár dynasty in Persia. (Náṣiri'd-Dín-Sháh had received from Bahá'u'lláh the most extensive and urgent Tablet of those sent to kings and rulers.)

28 November 1921	Death of ʿAbdu'l-Bahá at Haifa. By his *Will and Testament* his grandson Shoghi Effendi (1897–1957) is appointed Guardian of the Cause of God.
10 May 1925	Official acknowledgement of the Bahá'í Faith and its independence of Islám by the judgment of a court in Egypt (see p. 51).
9 June 1937–45	Dissolution of the Bahá'í community in Germany by the Nazi government, with prohibition of the Bahá'í Faith and destruction of its entire Bahá'í literature in Germany.
1937	On the initiative of Shoghi Effendi, in fulfilment of the 'Divine Plan' formulated by ʿAbdu'l-Bahá, the planned diffusion of the Bahá'í Faith over the whole world begins.
1953	There are twelve National Spiritual As-

	semblies and about 2,500 Bahá'í centres and communities throughout the world.
4 November 1957	Death of Shoghi Effendi. The 'Chief Stewards' of the Faith appointed by him—the 'Hands of the Cause of God'—continue work on the plan (the Ten Year Crusade) he had drawn up.
April 1963	Election in Haifa of the Universal House of Justice, the supreme legislative body of the Bahá'í Faith, by the members of the National Spiritual Assemblies of the world. A World Congress of Bahá'ís is held in London.
April 1967	The number of National Spiritual Assemblies has grown to 81, of Bahá'í centres and communities to 28,217, and Bahá'í literature has been translated into 397 languages. The number of countries opened to the Faith has reached 311, and Houses of Worship have been erected in four continents and Australasia.*
April 1975	The number of National Spiritual Assemblies has now grown to 119; there are approximately 72,000 Bahá'í centres and communities, and Bahá'í literature has been translated into 546 languages. The number of countries opened to the Faith has reached 330, and a Bahá'í House of Worship has been erected in Panama (dedicated 29 April 1972).

* The House of Worship in 'Ishqábád was razed in 1963 after damage by earthquake.

BIBLIOGRAPHY

'Abdu'l-Bahá. *Paris Talks*. London: Bahá'í Publishing Trust, 11th edn. 1969. (Published in the U.S.A. as *The Wisdom of 'Abdu'l-Bahá*.)
— *The Promulgation of Universal Peace*. Vol. I. Chicago: Bahai Temple Unity, 1922.
— *Some Answered Questions*. Trans. by Laura Clifford Barney. London: Bahá'í Publishing Trust, 1961. Wilmette: Bahá'í Publishing Trust, rev. edn. 1964.
Afrúkhtih, Dr. Yúnis Khán. *Kháṭirát-i-Nuh-Sáliy-i-'Akká*. (Memories of Nine Years in 'Akká.) Ṭihrán: 99 b.e. (a.d. 1942).
Bahá'í World, The. An International Record. New York: Bahá'í Publishing Committee, Vol. V, 1936. Haifa: The Universal House of Justice, Vol. XIII, 1970; Vol. XIV, 1974.
Bahá'í World Faith. Selected Writings of Bahá'u'lláh and 'Abdu'l-Bahá. Wilmette: Bahá'í Publishing Trust, 1943.
Bahá'u'lláh. *Daryáy-i-Dánish*. New Delhi: Bahá'í Publishing Trust.
— *Epistle to the Son of the Wolf*. Trans. by Shoghi Effendi. Wilmette: Bahá'í Publishing Trust, rev. edn. 1953.
— *Gleanings from the Writings of Bahá'u'lláh*. Trans. by Shoghi Effendi. Wilmette: Bahá'í Publishing Trust, 1935; rev. edn. 1952. London: Bahá'í Publishing Trust, 1949.
— *The Hidden Words*. Trans. by Shoghi Effendi. London: Bahá'í Publishing Trust, 1949. Wilmette: Bahá'í Publishing Trust, rev. edn. 1954.

— *The Kitáb-i-Íqán. The Book of Certitude*. Trans. by Shoghi Effendi. Wilmette: Bahá'í Publishing Trust, 2nd edn. 1950. London: Bahá'í Publishing Trust, 2nd edn. 1961.

— *The Seven Valleys and The Four Valleys*. Trans. by Ali-Kuli Khan (Nabílu'd-Dawlih), assisted by Marzieh Gail. Wilmette: Bahá'í Publishing Trust, rev. edn. 1952.

BALYUZI, H. M. *The Báb. The Herald of the Day of Days*. Oxford: George Ronald, 1973.

BAMM, PETER. *Frühe Stätten der Christenheit*. München: Kösel-Verlag, 1957. (Published in English as *Early Sites of Christianity*.)

BARNIKOL, E. *Der heilsgeschichtliche Jesus Christus*. Berlin: Evangelische Verlagsanstalt, 1960. Now published as *Das Leben Jesu in der Heilsgeschichte* by Veb Max Niemeyer Verlag Halle/Leipzig.

BARTH, KARL. *Der Römerbrief*. Zürich: Evangelischer Verlag, 1940. Zehnter Abdruck, 1967.

BERGMANN, GERHARD. *Alarm um die Bibel*. Gladbeck: Schriftenmissions-Verlag, 1961.

BLOMFIELD, LADY (Sitárih Khánum). *The Chosen Highway*. London: Bahá'í Publishing Trust, 1940. Wilmette: Bahá'í Publishing Trust, 1967.

BULTMANN, RUDOLF. *Zur Frage der Entmythologisierung*. München: R. Piper & Co. Verlag, 1954.

CONZELMANN, HANS. *Zur Methode der Leben-Jesu-Forschung*. München: Chr. Kaiser Verlag, 1967.

DESCHNER, KARL-HEINZ. *Abermals krähte der Hahn*. Stuttgart: Hans E. Günther Verlag, 1962.

ESSLEMONT, J. E. *Bahá'u'lláh and the New Era*. London: Bahá'í Publishing Trust, rev. edn. 1974.

GLASER, HERMANN. *Kleine Kulturgeschichte der Gegenwart*. Frankfurt-am-Main: Ullstein Taschenbuchverlag, 1959.

GRASS, HANS. *Ostergeschehen und Osterberichte*. Göttingen: Verlag Vandenhoeck & Ruprecht, 1956.
GROSS, JULIUS. *Entstehungsgeschichte des Erbsündendogmas*. München: Ernst Reinhardt Verlag, 1960.
HUNKE, SIGRID. *Allahs Sonne über dem Abendland*. Stuttgart: Deutsche Verlags-Anstalt, 1960. Frankfurt am Main and Hamburg: Fischer Bücherei, 1965.
JOCKEL, RUDOLF. *Islamische Geisteswelt*. Darmstadt: Holle-Verlag, 1954.
MU'AYYAD, DR. ḤABÍB. *Kháṭirát-i-Ḥabíb*. Tihrán: 1961.
MUMFORD, LEWIS. *The Transformations of Man*. New York: Harper & Row, Publishers, Inc., 1956. London: George Allen & Unwin Ltd., 1957.
NABÍL-I-AʿẒAM. *The Dawn-Breakers*. Wilmette: Bahá'í Publishing Trust, 1932. London: Bahá'í Publishing Trust, 1953.
NESTLE, WILHELM. *Die Krisis des Christentums*. Aalen: Scientia Antiquariat und Verlag, Schilling & Co., repr. 1974.
RUSSELL, BERTRAND. *Has Man a Future?* Harmondsworth: Penguin Books Ltd., 1961.
SARTORY, THOMAS. *Fragen an die Kirche*. München: Deutscher Taschenbuch Verlag, 1965.
SCHNEIDER, CARL. *Geistesgeschichte des Antiken Christentums*. München: C. H. Beck'sche Verlagsbuchhandlung, 1954.
SCHOEPS, HANS-JOACHIM. *Paulus Die Theologie des Apostels im Lichte der Judischen Religionsgeschichte*. Tübingen: J. C. B. Mohr Verlag, 1959. (Published in English as *Paul, The Theology of the Apostle in the Light of Jewish Religious History*.)
SCHREY, HEINZ-HORST. *Weltbild und Glaube im 20. Jahrhundert*. Göttingen: Verlag Vandenhoeck & Ruprecht, 1961.
SCHWEITZER, ALBERT. *The Mysticism of Paul the Apostle*.

Trans. from the German by William Montgomery. London: A. & C. Black Ltd., 1931.

SEARS, WILLIAM. *Thief in the Night*. London: George Ronald, rev. edn. 1964.

SEIGNOBOS, CH. *Histoire de la Civilisation au Moyen Age*. Paris: G. Masson, 1887. (Published in English as *History of Medieval Civilization*.)

SHOGHI EFFENDI. *God Passes By*. Wilmette: Bahá'í Publishing Trust, 1944.

— *The Promised Day is Come*. Wilmette: Bahá'í Publishing Trust, repr. 1961.

— *The World Order of Bahá'u'lláh*. Wilmette: Bahá'í Publishing Trust, 1938; rev. edn. 1955.

SHOGHI EFFENDI and SITARIH KHANUM (Lady Blomfield). *The Passing of 'Abdu'l-Baha*. Stuttgart: 1922.

SZCZESNY, GERHARD. *The Future of Unbelief*. Trans. from the German by Edward B. Gardside. New York: George Braziller, Inc., 1961. London: Heinemann (William) Ltd., 1962.

TOYNBEE, ARNOLD. *Christianity among the Religions of the World*. London: Oxford University Press, 1958.

— *Civilization on Trial*. London: Oxford University Press, 1948.

WHITEHEAD, ALFRED NORTH. *Science and the Modern World*. New York: Macmillan Publishing Co., Inc., 1925. London: Cambridge University Press, 1926.

REFERENCES

Full details of authors and titles are given in the bibliography. The references give the surname of the author only, but an abbreviated title is added if more than one title is listed for that author. The Authorized Version of the Bible is used throughout the book, as is Rodwell's translation of the Koran (Qur'án).

CHAPTER I: HAS RELIGION FAILED?

1. Bahá'u'lláh, *Gleanings*, section cxxxii.
2. See Sartory, p. 29.
3. Mark xiii, 21.
4. See Conzelmann, p. 8.
5. Grass, p. 225. Translated by Hélène Momtaz Neri.
6. E. Troeltsch, cited by Bergmann, p. 22.
7. Barnikol, p. 581.
8. Szczesny, p. 133 (U.S. edn.).
9. *Acta Apostolicae Sedis*, 1 July 1961, vol. LIII, p. 360.
10. See Isaiah xl, 22, and Psalms civ, 2.
11. See Barth.
12. Schrey, p. 43.
13. See Bultmann.
14. I Corinthians iv, 5, and ii, 7–11.
15. Daniel xii, 8–9.
16. Dr. E. Müller-Gangloff, 'Revolution des Christentums?', a talk given on 1 March 1959 on Süddeutschen Rundfunk.
17. II Peter iii, 10.
18. *ibid.*, v. 13.
19. See Revelation ii, 17; iii, 12; xix, 11–16; and Isaiah, lxii, 2.
20. Arnold Toynbee, 'Perspektiven der Welt von morgen', an address given on 24 November 1965 at the University of Cologne.
21. Cited by William S. Hatcher in *World Order*, A Bahá'í Magazine, Winter 1966, p. 26.

CHAPTER II: THE RELIGION OF UNITY

1. Shoghi Effendi, *World Order*, p. 97.

2. The reader is referred to Esslemont, chs. 9 and 10, for a fuller discussion of these principles.
3. Bahá'u'lláh, *Daryáy-i-Dánish*, p. 106.
4. Toynbee, *Civilization on Trial*, pp. 235–6; also, pp. 39–40, 55, 91.

CHAPTER III: THE OTHER FUTURE

1. Bahá'u'lláh, *Gleanings*, sec. xliii.
2. Cited *Bahá'í World Faith*, p. 183.
3. Cited by Blomfield, p. 184.
4. Russell, pp. 49–50. Reprinted by permission of Penguin Books Ltd.
5. *ibid.*, pp. 70–1, for Dr. Pauling's statement. (*The Humanist*, March–April 1961.) Those by the Defence Secretary and H. Kahn appear on pp. 29 and 36.
6. *ibid.*, p. 36. Reprinted by permission of Penguin Books Ltd.
7. Mumford, p. 181 (U.S. edn.); p. 140 (Brit. edn.).
8. Bahá'u'lláh, *Gleanings*, sec. cxviii.
9. *ibid.*, lxx.
10. See the booklet by Ugo R. Giachery, *One God, One Truth, One People*, 'Some Thoughts on the Peace Encyclical of Pope John XXIII', (Wilmette: Bahá'í Publishing Trust, 1971).
11. Matthew viii, 28, and Mark vi, 3.
12. An essay entitled 'Constructive Religion', *The Bahá'í World*, vol. VIII, p. 772.

CHAPTER IV: 'THE WALLS THAT DIVIDE US . . .'

1. John xiv, 2.
2. Qur'án ii, 130.
3. *ibid.* iii, 1–2.
4. Bamm, pp. 260 and 222. Translated by Oliver Coburn.
5. See Hunke, pp. 219 and 214 ff. (Deutsche Verlags-Anstalt edn.), for some of the facts in this paragraph.
6. *ibid.*, pp. 114 ff.
7. *ibid.*, p. 115.
8. *ibid.*, p. 119 (Fischer edn.)
9. Qur'án xxxix, 12.
10. Cited by Hunke, p. 169 (Deutsche Verlags-Anstalt edn.).
11. Cited by Jockel, p. 75.
12. Cited by Hunke, p. 199 (D.V.-A. edn.).
13. Seignobos, pp. 58–9. Translated by Mary K. Perkins.
14. Qur'án ii, 186.
15. *The Christian Century*, 10 April 1957.

16. Shoghi Effendi, *World Order*, pp. 152, 156.
17. Mumford, p. 86 (U.S. edn.); p. 68 (Brit. edn.).
18. Genesis i, 3.
19. Bahá'u'lláh, *Gleanings*, sec. xcix.
20. *Bahá'í World Faith*, p. 251.
21. John v, 46.
22. Toynbee, *Christianity among the Religions of the World*, p. 104.
23. Bahá'u'lláh, *Gleanings*, sec. lxxxviii.
24. Shoghi Effendi, *God Passes By*, p. 365.
25. From a written statement made at the request of the author, when a student of Professor von Glasenapp.
26. Bahá'u'lláh, *Gleanings*, sec. cxxix.
27. Cited by Shoghi Effendi, *World Order*, pp. 115–16.
28. John xiv, 2.

Chapter V: The New Earth

1. Bahá'u'lláh, *Gleanings*, sec. xliii.
2. Glaser, p. 10.
3. Genesis i, 28; ii, 19.
4. *ibid.* i, 26.
5. Bahá'u'lláh, *Hidden Words* (Persian), no. 27.
6. Cited by Shoghi Effendi, *World Order*, p. 112.
7. See Bahá'u'lláh, *Kitáb-i-Íqán*, p. 243 (U.S. edn.); p. 155 (Brit. edn.).
8. Cited by Shoghi Effendi, *World Order*, p. 103.
9. Bahá'u'lláh, *Gleanings*, sec. xiv.
10. Shoghi Effendi, *World Order*, pp. 203–4.

Chapter VI: The Herald

1. Cited by Shoghi Effendi, *God Passes By*, pp. 5–6. See also Nabíl-i-A'ẓam, pp. 62, 65 (U.S. edn.); pp. 43, 44 (Brit. edn.).
2. *ibid.*, p. 76.
3. *ibid.*, p. 21.
4. *ibid.*, p. 52.
5. *idem.*
6. *ibid.*, p. 53.
7. F.O. 60/152. The document is quoted by Balyuzi, appendix 2.
8. *The Bahá'í World*, vol. XIV, p. 562.
9. Shoghi Effendi, *God Passes By*, pp. 54–5.
10. Bahá'u'lláh, *Gleanings*, sec. i.
11. *ibid.*, sec. xxiv.
12. Cited *The Bahá'í World*, vol. XIII, p. 804.

REFERENCES

13. *ibid.*, p. 818, for the original French; see Shoghi Effendi, *God Passes By*, p. 375, for English translation.
14. *ibid.*, p. 817. Letter to Frid ul Khan Wadelbekow. Second quotation cited by Martha Root, *The Bahá'í World*, vol. V, p. 563.
15. Shoghi Effendi, *God Passes By*, p. 412.

CHAPTER VII: GOD'S COVENANT FULFILLED

1. For further details see Shoghi Effendi, *God Passes By*, chap. 5.
2. Bahá'u'lláh, *Gleanings*, sec. xiv.
3. *ibid.*, sec. cv. The excerpts have been rearranged.
4. Cited by Shoghi Effendi, *God Passes By*, p. 187.
5. Afrúkhtih, pp. 148–9, 162; and Mu'ayyad, pp. 218–19.
6. Shoghi Effendi, *World Order*, p. 134.
7. Cited by Shoghi Effendi, *The Passing of 'Abdu'l-Baha*, p. 18.
8. 'Abdu'l-Bahá, *Promulgation*, vol. I, p. 89.

CHAPTER VIII: CHRIST

1. Qur'án cxii.
2. *ibid.* xxi, 26–9.
3. *ibid.* ix, 30–1.
4. *ibid.* xix, 91–7.
5. John i, 12–13.
6. Bahá'u'lláh, *Gleanings*, sec. xxvi.
7. John xiv, 9–10.
8. *ibid.* v. 24.
9. *ibid.* v. 28.
10. Mark x, 18.
11. *ibid.* xiii, 32.
12. See Shaykh Ahmad-i-Ahsá'í in *Sharhu'z-Ziyárat* (Ṭihrán: 1267 A.H., or A.D. 1851), pp. 106 and 175. This station of the Manifestations of God is apostrophized in Islamic theology as the station of Tawḥíd (Unity), and finds its expression in the following tradition which is recorded in the prayer for the month of Rajab: 'There is no difference between Thee (God) and them (Manifestations of God), except that they are Thy servants and creatures'. (pp. 107 and 179.)
13. Bahá'u'lláh, *Gleanings*, sec. xxxi.
14. Shaykh Ahmad-i-Ahsá'í, *op. cit.*, pp. 186, 31. See also Majlisí, *Biháru'l-Anwár*, vol. VII, and Shaykh Yúsuf-i-Bahrání, *Anísu'l-Khátir* (*Kashkúl-i-Bahrání*). These traditions are cited by Bahá'u'lláh in *Kitáb-i-Íqán*, p. 153 (U.S. edn.), pp. 98–9 (Brit. edn.).
15. John viii, 58 and xiv, 6.

16. *ibid.* i, 19–21.
17. Matthew xvii, 10–13.
18. John xvi, 12–13.
19. From an essay entitled 'For Christian Contacts'. British *Bahá'í Journal*, No. 117.
20. Bahá'u'lláh, *Gleanings*, sec. cxxiv.
21. *ibid.*, sec. xciv.
22. Cited by Bahá'u'lláh, *The Seven Valleys*, p. 23.
23. John xiv, 6.
24. Bahá'u'lláh, *Gleanings*, sec. xix.
25. *ibid.*, sec. xx.
26. 'Abdu'l-Bahá, *Some Answered Questions*, chap. lxvii.
27. 'Abdu'l-Bahá, *Paris Talks*, p. 24.
28. Bahá'u'lláh, *Gleanings*, sec. cxxii.
29. *ibid.*, sec. ci.
30. *ibid.*, sec. lxxxii.
31. Luke xviii, 8.
32. I Corinthians iv, 5.
33. Bahá'u'lláh, *Gleanings*, sec. xxiii.
34. Shoghi Effendi, *Promised Day*, p. 113.
35. 'Abdu'l-Bahá, *Some Answered Questions*, chap. xxvii.
36. Gross, vol. I, p. 50.
37. *ibid.*, p. 375.
38. Cited by Deschner, p. 57.
39. Schneider, vol. I, p. 236.
40. Acts xiv, 11–12.
41. Schweitzer, p. 173.
42. Nestle, p. 89.
43. Schoeps, p. 278.
44. Deschner, p. 180.
45. 'Abdu'l-Bahá, *Some Answered Questions*, chap. xxix.
46. *idem.* This and the preceding quotation are in explanation of I Corinthians xv, 22.
47. *ibid.* chap. xviii.
48. Sartory, p. 43.
49. Bahá'u'lláh, *Gleanings*, sec. xxxvi.

Chapter IX: The New Heaven

1. Cited by Shoghi Effendi, *Promised Day*, pp. 30–1.
2. Cited by Deschner, p. 26.
3. Matthew xxiv, 29–31.
4. Mark xiii, 21.

REFERENCES

5. Mumford, pp. 182–3 (U.S. edn.); pp. 140–1 (Brit. edn.).
6. Cited by Shoghi Effendi, *Promised Day*, p. 105.
7. Matthew xxiv, 30. See also Luke xxi, 27.
8. II Peter iii, 10.
9. Luke xxi, 34–5.
10. *ibid.* xvii, 20.
11. Matthew xxiv, 27.
12. Bahá'u'lláh, *Gleanings*, sec. ci.
13. Whitehead, pp. 233–4.
14. John vi, 38.
15. *ibid.* iii, 13.
16. *ibid.* i, 23. See also Matthew iii, 3 and Mark i, 3.
17. *ibid.* i, 46.
18. Bahá'u'lláh, *Kitáb-i-Íqán*, pp. 42, 38 (U.S. edn.); pp. 25–8 (Brit. edn.).
19. Matthew viii, 22.
20. Bahá'u'lláh, *Kitáb-i-Íqán*, p. 107 (U.S. edn.); p. 69 (Brit. edn.).
21. Bahá'u'lláh, *Gleanings*, sec. xvii.
22. Shoghi Effendi, *God Passes By*, pp. 94–6 (rearranged).
23. See Sears, *Thief in the Night*.
24. 'Abdu'l-Bahá, *Some Answered Questions*, chap. xl.
25. Cited by Shoghi Effendi, *God Passes By*, p. 101.
26. *ibid.*, p. 102.
27. *idem.*

Lewis and Clark College - Watzek Library
BP365 .S2813   wmain
Sabet, Huschmand/The heavens are cleft a

3 5209 00385 8707